BRIDGES: Activity Guide and Assessment Options

To Accompany

EFFECTIVE TEACHING METHODS
Fifth Edition

by
Gary D. Borich

Prepared by Debra Bayles Martin

PEARSON
Merrill
Prentice Hall

Upper Saddle River, New Jersey
Columbus, Ohio

Vice President and Executive Publisher: Jeffery W. Johnston
Executive Editor: Debra Stollenwerk
Editorial Assistant: Mary Morrill
Development Editor: Kimberly J. Lundy
Production Editor: Kris Robinson-Roach
Production Coordination: WordCrafters
Design Coordinator: Diane C. Lorenzo
Cover Designer: Jim Hunter
Cover Image: Getty One
Production Manager: Pamela Bennett
Director of Marketing: Ann Castel Davis
Marketing Manager: Darcy Betts Prybella
Marketing Coordinator: Tyra Poole

10 9 8 7 6 5 4 3 2

ISBN: 0-13-114552-5

Contents

Introduction

Welcome to *BRIDGES*, an instructional device specially designed for instructors and students using *Effective Teaching Methods, Fifth Edition*. BRIDGES represents a new concept in textbook supplements—providing instructors and students the same lesson plans and activity ideas. This supplement features updated activities and references and a more extensive children's literature bibliography for connecting course concepts to discussions of read-aloud books. As you consider the unique format of *BRIDGES*, questions like these may arise:

Q: **Is *BRIDGES* a Teacher Guide or a Student Manual?**

A: Both. A traditional view of learning suggests that a teacher "teaches" information to students who "learn" it. Instructional supplements created with this view generally provide material for a teacher to share with students and/or activities for students to complete for the teacher. However, a constructivist view of learning suggests that students (and teachers) learn through interaction with people and materials, constructing their own personal meanings. In such a view, knowledge is not something a teacher "transmits" to a student. Thus, working from the *BRIDGES* guide, instructors and students "start on the same page" to understand learning and teaching together, from the inside out. Students experience various strategies "as learners," and also "as teachers"—seeing from the guide how specific activities are designed and implemented, and later evaluating their effectiveness for specific purposes.

Q: **What's the best way to use *BRIDGES*?**

A: How you use *BRIDGES* depends on your teaching experience and philosophy. For example, course instructors may want to peruse the complete guide before a course begins and select specific activities to highlight in class. They may choose from among activities within a chapter, experimenting with various individual and group assignments. These learning activities can and should be viewed as experiments—and can be evaluated after their use. Related ideas and cross-references among chapters can be added as well. For example, an activity suggested in Chapter 2 may also apply to another chapter. Course instructors may also invite student input. Students can peruse the suggestions for a particular chapter and suggest activities in which they'd like to participate. They may also work on their own and select from the guide specific activities to enhance personal and small group study.

Q: **How do I assess the effectiveness of *BRIDGES* activities?**

A: The approach for course assessment varies according to the *BRIDGES* activities used in class. For example, instructors who generally implement whole class instructional approaches may desire to evaluate student progress using the true/false, multiple choice, and matching questions provided for each chapter. Those who adopt a performance assessment focus may require that students complete a personal portfolio containing a predetermined number of learning and assessment activities suggested in *BRIDGES*. These products may be supplemented with simple explanation sheets detailing why a particular product was selected for the portfolio, what was learned from the activity, and how it might apply to future learning/teaching. Other assessment ideas are also provided for each chapter.

Q: **Doesn't giving the students a copy of the Teacher's Guide detract from the freshness of the course presentation?**

A: While the answer to this question will depend largely upon your point of view, it is our belief that allowing students to see the plans from which an instructor works provides an important window on the teaching process—offering a model of how to plan and implement instruction that is often mentioned but rarely demonstrated to students. Students who are informed about possible educational interventions from which an instructor chooses, who are allowed to experience those interventions as learners, and who are allowed to share their insights about the effects of those interventions are likely to feel valued for their own expertise as learners, better internalize subtleties of particular strategies, and inform instructors of important modifications for future teaching. This dual stance on the part of instructors and students (taking both a participatory and an evaluative view) can encourage the kind of thinking necessary for reflective teaching. Further, students who see how their instructor "teaches" a course will likely gain a greater understanding of how they themselves might model specific strategies in their future classrooms.

Q: **So who's the teacher in this course?**

A: If coming to know involves constructing a personal meaning, then everyone involved in this course is both a student at times and a teacher at others. The "student" is the person who encounters something new and attempts to "fit" it into his or her existing understanding. The "teacher" is the person

sharing a particular insight or idea at any given moment. This open sharing is not, however, an excuse for instructors to yield to majority rule or devalue their own experience or expertise. While a student-centered focus in instruction allows students to contribute to the learning experience, the instructor's role still remains one of guidance—there are some ideas and concepts which are more important and helpful than others, and judgments (about what to focus on) should remain within the instructor's purview.

Q: **When should we read the chapters in *Effective Teaching Methods?***

A: *BRIDGES* activities are generally written as if the chapter content has been read by all participants before the class meets. However, some ideas may be more effective if used before reading occurs. Additionally, some students develop strong preferences about when to read text chapters (i.e., before or after the topic is addressed in class). Instructors should peruse activity suggestions far enough in advance of a particular chapter to notify students of their preferences about when a specific chapter (or part of a chapter) should be read.

Q: **How does the format of *BRIDGES* work? What is the thinking/purpose behind each category?**

A: Instructional suggestions for each chapter are presented in chart form. Other related information appears under bold-faced headings. A sample chart with activity descriptions and references follows on pages vii–xi.

Chapter Number	A. *Personal, Dialogue, or Buddy Journals*	B. *Self-Directed Study Activities*	C. *Cooperative & Collaborative Ideas*	D. *Whole Class*
Introducing the Content Assimilating/ Reviewing the Content	The purpose of journal writing is to encourage students (and the instructor) to connect course concepts with personal experiences. As students express their views, they enhance their expressive capacity. Further, the process of translating mental ideas to written text can help crystalize vague ideas and reveal areas where understanding is incomplete. **DIALOGUE JOURNALS*** are generally written between the student and the instructor, **BUDDY JOURNALS** are exchanged between two student partners, and **SELF-REFLECTIVE JOURNALS** may be kept in a more traditional "diary" sense—wherein each student writes to himself/herself as the primary audience.	Ideas in this column encourage students to go beyond course requirements and extend their own learning. These activities provide students the freedom to work on projects at their own pace, to explore topics of interest, and to share their discoveries. The work completed in this area can be as public or as private as students desire. Indeed, some of it (or perhaps all) may never be made public.	As students interact with peers, they come to better understand one another and draw upon others' strengths to enhance their own thinking. Through carefully structured social interaction, the ability to work with others improves—yielding a sense of belonging and collegiality—which is important for affective growth and development. Throughout the course, students may work with the same partner and/or small group to achieve a sense of stability. Or, they can work with a variety of partners and small groups to gain even more experience interacting. Activities in this column should also enhance learning enjoyment as students engage in a variety of tasks, from writing song lyrics and poetry to summarizing key issues, completing art projects, etc.	Because students may come from a number of communities, they may share more differences than similarities when this course begins. As students experience course concepts and strategies together, they build a base of common experience from which to draw future examples and to support future learning. These shared experiences also build unity, broaden perspectives, and engender a sense of "groupness" and accepted norms.

*See both **"SUGGESTED READINGS"** and **"ACTIVE LEARNING"** at the end of this chapter for further information about journals.

Checking Your Understanding

This is the only section of the manual in which instructor and student copies differ. While students receive the questions and answers for 10–15 practice questions per chapter, instructors receive an additional 15–20 questions and answers for use in generating a test students have not previously seen. While practice questions are not intended to "teach to the test," they do provide an example for students of the kinds of questions to expect on a traditional test, as well as suggest topic areas for test review. Teachers may want to use some practice questions in their tests along with questions from the **TEST BANK.**

Note: In cases where traditional assessment is used, it can be adapted to allow for more student input by inviting student clarification. For example, students can write in question clarifications to explain an answer. These comments can be taken into consideration in the event a student "misses" an answer—acknowledging the possibility of alternative views and readings of questions. Another adaptation requires students to underline and correct the false part of a true/false question to receive full credit for a correct response.

Performance Assessment Ideas

Individual	*Small Group*	*Whole Class*
This section contains suggestions for performance assessments which can be undertaken by individuals to enhance their own learning or which can be assigned by the instructor. Its goal is to enhance the application of chapter concepts to real life teaching issues and situations.	Since teachers often work in collaborative groups to evaluate curriculum and make school decisions, ideas in this section are designed to encourage cooperation and collaboration, rather than individual competitiveness. Students are evaluated not only on the quality of the group product but on the quality of group participation and interaction. Careful debriefing of these experiences can help students enhance their social and leadership skills along with their understanding of course content.	This section includes assessment options for involving the students in whole group work. Sometimes the ideas involve assignments which students compile to create a "class" product. Other times, the ideas involve every student in the same experience. This differs from the first column of performance assessment ideas in that all students are required to complete a particular activity, rather than only a few. However, ideas found in Column 1 (and even Column 2) can often be interchanged with those in this column and instructors are encouraged to implement suggestions flexibly.

CHILDREN'S LITERATURE CONNECTION

Although children's literature is often regarded as something to be read and enjoyed only by young children, many college and university instructors have found it a valuable resource for illustrating complex concepts for older audiences. Thus, this section includes children's literature sources which support course content in novel or entertaining ways. Instructors may choose to read aloud from these sources to introduce or illustrate a topic and then discuss implications with the class—or they may ask students to share from the sources and summarize connections they find between the literature and the course.

SUGGESTED READINGS

These annotated references support individual study for chapter activities and concepts. For example, the following references deal with the use of journals and with reconceptualizing the way university classes are designed:

Anderson, J. (1992/1993). Journal writing: The promise and the reality. *Journal of Reading, 36*(4), 304–9.
Addresses problems with journal writing such as overuse, ethics, goals, and grading. Suggests ways to make journals a useful pleasure.
Bromley, K. (1990). Buddy journals make the reading-writing connection. *The Reading Teacher, 43*(2), 122–9.
Describes the use and advantages of buddy journals.
Edwards, P. R. (1991/1992). Using dialectical journals to teach thinking skills. *Journal of Reading, 35*(4), 312–6.
Discusses various types of journals, how to introduce them, and how to use them to encourage students' thinking skills.
Menon, R. (1994, June). Using mathematics journals more effectively. *Mathematics Teaching,* 18–9.
Suggests some considerations for using journals in teaching mathematics.
Stewart, C., & Chance, L. (1995). Making connections: Journal writing and the Professional Teaching Standards. *The Mathematics Teacher, 88*(2), 92–5.
Describes numerous ways journal writing supports mathematics instruction as well as development of other skills. Discusses both teacher and student roles in journal writing.
Tinto, V. (1997). Enhancing learning via community. *Thought & Action, 13*(1), 53–8.
Suggests that creating learning communities at the university level is a positive and useful way to enhance collegiate learning.
Wells, M. C. (1992/1993). At the junction of reading and writing: How dialogue journals contribute to students' reading development. *Journal of Reading, 36*(4), 294–302.
A teacher studies her students' dialogue journals to determine their effect on reading development. The article includes excerpts of student entries and categories into which entries fell, along with the author's conclusions about those categories.

ACTIVE LEARNING

Methods courses are often criticized for "telling" students about approaches rather than "showing" them. To address this important concern, instructions are included in this section for completing activities in this course that can later be used in elementary and secondary teaching. Thus, students experience in this course as learners instructional strategies they can later use in their own teaching. These activities appear by name in the chapter charts, along with a page number where they are described in detail. When applicable, related articles are footnoted to the activities as well.

For example, on the first day of the college course, the instructor may invite students to complete the **WRITTEN CONVERSATION** activity explained below. This activity helps students "break the ice" on the first day and share important insights. With small adaptations, **WRITTEN CONVERSATION** can also be used by the students later when they begin teaching. Activities included throughout *BRIDGES* reflect this dual focus. They are suggested both as vehicles for college students to use now in learning course content—and as effective teaching strategies for college students to use later in teaching their own students.

WRITTEN CONVERSATION (College Adaptation)

Place students in pairs (through random assignment or by allowing them to choose someone they do not know well). Ask each student to write his or her name at the top of a blank piece of paper. Tell students that the goal of this activity is for them to discover interesting facts about one another through written conversation. As the activity begins, Student 1 writes a question for Student 2 on Student 2's paper. Student 3 does the same for Student 1. Once the question is written, they exchange papers to respond to the question in writing. Papers are then exchanged again so that a second question for Student 2 is written on Student 2's paper and vice versa. No talking is allowed during this "written conversation." Encourage students to ask not only common questions (e.g., What is your name? Why are you enrolled in this course?), but to ask creative questions (e.g., "What animal are you most like and why? What was the most exciting adventure in your life?). After approximately 5 minutes, ask students to choose two interesting insights from the interview and share them as they introduce their partners to the class.

Note: An effective extension of **WRITTEN CONVERSATION** for the first day of this course involves asking questions such as the following:

What is an effective teacher?
How long does it take to become an effective teacher?

How do you become one?
Is there only one definition of an effective teacher?

WRITTEN CONVERSATION (Elementary Adaptation)

For very young students, the teacher begins: 1) by writing questions on the chalkboard that students answer at their desks or, 2) asking questions orally. Next, students ask the questions of one another and write or draw the responses on their papers. Students are paired and ask such questions as:

What is your name?	How old are you?	What is your favorite color?
What is your favorite food?	Do you have pets?	What do you like to do?

As above, students introduce their partners to the class and share 2–3 insights. The teacher may also take a photo of each student and add it to the "final" copy of the interview answers. This is displayed in class so students can read about each other.

JOURNALS

Journal writing encourages reflective thinking and allows students to connect personal experiences with course content. As one approach to journal writing, **PERSONAL JOURNALS** provide a safe and private avenue for student thinking—but their "diary-like" quality can also decrease their effectiveness if students fail to grasp their value, writing irregular or insincere entries. A second approach involves **DIALOGUE JOURNALS,** which allow the instructor to interact with each student on a one-to-one basis, reading and responding personally to students' emerging understandings and questions. Although the idea of responding in writing to each student can be overwhelming, instructors generally find that by responding to a few journals each day they can address each student at least once a week. While such responses require some out-of-class time to complete, benefits include the opportunity to answer students' questions as they arise and to gain insight into each student's unique perspective on course material. **BUDDY JOURNALS** fall somewhere between the privacy of personal journals and the instructor-student interaction of dialogue journals. Students address entries to a specified "buddy" in the class with whom they "correspond" daily. Buddy journals encourage student interaction and processing of course material, but provide the instructor less opportunity to engage directly in student processing (unless the instructor participates as someone's buddy).

Instructors may rely upon a particular journal approach throughout the semester, or may alternate approaches at various junctures. It is important that students know which type of journal they will be writing so that they can address their comments to an appropriate audience. Throughout the course, students should be encouraged to share personal insights from any type of journal used. Instructors should also write journal entries and share their own insights and/or struggles periodically.

Q: How should I begin the course?
A: You may want to adapt a general schedule from the timetables detailed below:

60 minute meeting time

Provide materials for students to make name tags as they enter. Ask them to place their name tags on the desks/tables each day for the first several days of class. You may also want students to complete (and hand in) the **INTEREST INVENTORY** (see p. xiii) so you can come to know your students better. This can be done as students enter, may be assigned for "homework," or can be completed on another day.

10 minutes	Introduce yourself, the course goals, and the general course outline. Take attendance if desired.
10 minutes	Distribute a course syllabus, highlight key issues, ask students to read it through on their own.
5 minutes	Read aloud from a children's literature source, current teaching magazine article, etc.
25 minutes	Complete the **WRITTEN CONVERSATION** activity (see p. x) to introduce students to one another and prepare for a discussion on teacher effectiveness
10 minutes	If time permits and you have chosen to use journals, introduce the idea and ask students to write a short journal entry. If not, make closing comments and dismiss the class.

90 minute meeting time

Complete the first 50 minutes as outlined on the 60 minute schedule above. Follow the schedule below for the remaining 40 minutes.

30 minutes	Begin an introductory lecture, working from students' responses to the questions during the **WRITTEN CONVERSATION** activity and from suggestions on page 1–4 of this guide.
10 minutes	If time permits and you have chosen to use journals, introduce the idea and ask students to write a short journal entry. If not, make closing comments and dismiss the class.

Once the course is going, you may want to follow the schedules below:

60 minute meeting time

10 minutes	Journal entry in response to a probe question or read aloud to introduce the day's topic.
25 minutes	Lecture/Input.
20 minutes	Small group activity to reinforce concept.
5 minutes	Summarize and close.

90 minute meeting time

10 minutes	Journal or read aloud.
35 minutes	Lecture/Input.
30 minutes	Small group activity to reinforce concept.
10 minutes	Journal or read aloud (whichever was not completed at the beginning of class).
5 minutes	Summarize and close.

Interest Inventory

My full name is _____

_____.

My friends call me _____.

My birthday is _____.

I have _____ brothers and _____ sisters. They range

in age from _____ years to _____ years.

My hair is _____ and my eyes are _____.

My favorite friend is _____

because _____.

The season of the year I like best is _____.

I like this season best because that is when _____

_____.

My favorite day of the week is _____.

I like it because _____

_____.

One thing I do well is _____

_____.

One thing I'd like to do better is _____

because _____.

My experience with young children and adults includes _____

_____.

If I could have/do anything in the world, it would be_____

_____ because

_____.

My favorite color is _____.

My favorite book is _____

_____.

I like it because _____.

When I have free time, I like to _____

_____.

My favorite subject in school is/was _____

_____ because

_____.

My pet peeve is _____.

because _____

_____.

Something I like about school is _____

_____.

Something I don't like about school is _____

_____.

I want to be a _____ because

_____.

BRIDGES

**Chapter 1
The Effective Teacher**

Chapter 1	A. *Personal, Dialogue, or Buddy Journals*	B. *Self-Directed Study Activities*	C. *Cooperative & Collaborative Ideas*	D. *Whole Class*
Introducing the Content	1. **THINK** about a favorite teacher. How did s/he act, look, teach? Why was this teacher a favorite? Did this person influence your career choice?* 2. What makes an effective teacher? What do you **REMEMBER** about an effective or ineffective teacher you knew? What made him/her this way?	1. Complete the practice test questions at the end of this chapter as an **ANTICIPATION GUIDE** (p. 3).[1] Read the chapter and then answer the questions a second time. How did your answers change? Share your experience with the class—how did it enhance your reading or involve you more in the chapter?	1. What does it mean for a teacher to be flexible? What are some memories you have of flexible or inflexible teachers? What happened? Was the outcome good or bad? Why do you feel that way? Share your responses using the cooperative learning strategy **THINK, PAIR, SHARE** (p. 7).[2]	1. **CREATE** and **DISPLAY AN OVERHEAD TRANSPARENCY** printed with the words "Portrait of a Perfect Teacher" and a drawing of a male or female person. With the class, **BRAINSTORM** attributes of a "perfect" or "effective" teacher. **MAP** or **WEB** (pp. 7–8)[3] these traits on the chalkboard or a blank overhead transparency. Encourage interaction, especially among those who differ in perspective.

*Students will need to know which type of journal they will be keeping so that they can address their comments to an appropriate audience (see p. xi).
[1,2,3]These numbers are keyed to the references and activities at the end of each chapter.

Chapter 1 continued	A. Personal, Dialogue, or Buddy Journals	B. Self-Directed Study Activities	C. Cooperative & Collaborative Ideas	D. Whole Class
Assimilating/ Reviewing the Content	3. **REFLECT** on a time you were praised and compare it to a time when someone extended your thinking. What were some of the affective and academic results? What differences do you see between praise and extension of thinking? 4. **REFLECT** on an unspoken classroom dialogue you remember. What seemed to be happening? What impression did you form of the participants? What conclusions did you draw?	2. **WRITE** a one- or two-sentence SUMMARY for this chapter on the top of this page to help you remember important content at a glance. You may want to do this for every chapter as a helpful device. 3. **SELECT** and **READ** an article for the Suggested Readings section of this guide (pp. 5–6). **WRITE** a **SHORT SUMMARY** of the article and reflect on how it supports or challenges the material in Chapter 1 of your text.	2. Work in groups to **BRAINSTORM** ways to praise/motivate students. Think also of ways a teacher might extend short answers given by students. **SHARE** your lists with the class, and if desired, compile one class list. 3. In small groups, **ROLE PLAY** the use of praise in several impromptu student-teacher interactions. Reenact the scenarios, replacing praise with extension comments. Choose a scenario and **PERFORM** both the praise and the extension versions for the class. 4. **DISCUSS WITH A PARTNER** why teacher affect might be more important in low SES classrooms.	2. As a group, **BRAINSTORM** a definition of teaching. How does this definition relate to the discussion of the "perfect" or "effective" teacher in Activity 1-D-1 above? **COMPARE** your class definition of teaching with that in the text. How is your definition similar? How does it differ?

Chapter 1: Checking Your Understanding

True or False:

1. _____ The degree of a student's engagement with a learning task is obvious.

2. _____ If students generally complete school tasks at moderate to high rates of success, they will probably grow bored in class and suffer from a negative attitude.

3. _____ "Chapter 1" schools are those in which students have many economic and educational advantages.

4. _____ Teachers need a ready vocabulary of praise words to acknowledge and reward student effort. Some of the best of these words are: "good," "correct," and "right."

5. _____ One of the most important abilities teachers must develop is the ability to be flexible—to sense when a change from one emphasis to another is necessary.

6. _____ Studying the practices used by effective teachers is necessary to becoming an effective teacher.

7. _____ A role model definition of effective teaching followed attempts to identify psychological characteristics of effective teachers (e.g., personality, attitude, experience, and aptitude and/or achievement).

8. _____ What a teacher doesn't say is every bit as important as what a teacher does say.

9. _____ A teacher's employment experience (other than teaching) predicts little of his or her day-to-day classroom effectiveness.

10. _____ Research has identified specific teacher behaviors which consistently relate to desirable student performance.

11. _____ Teachers should ask questions for which there is a single "right" answer most of the time.

12. _____ There is a large body of research about the effects of SES (socioeconomic status) on the educational achievement of students at the secondary level.

13. _____ Students feel important and are encouraged to participate in class when a teacher uses their ideas in moving a class lecture or activity forward.

14. _____ Effective teachers use careful language such as "might be" or "could possibly happen" to avoid overstating lesson ideas.

15. _____ Effective teachers use students' responses and ideas in a number of ways to enhance classroom environment and student learning.

16. _____ Process questions help students use their own knowledge to think more deeply about a concept.

17. _____ Extremely enthusiastic teachers are most effective in encouraging student achievement.

18. _____ Teachers typically progress through three stages of concern in their careers.

| 1. F | 2. F | 3. F | 4. F | 5. T | 6. T | 7. T | 8. F | 9. T |
| 10. T | 11. F | 12. F | 13. T | 14. F | 15. T | 16. T | 17. F | 18. T |

Chapter 1: Performance Assessment Ideas		
Individual	*Small Group*	*Whole Class*
1. **REFER BACK** to your journal entry for Activity 1-A-2. What traits did you list in your description of an effective teacher? How many of these traits are mentioned in Chapter 1 of your text? Are there traits you would add to that list? Delete? Why? **SUPPORT** your views with appropriate sources (including personal experience, text passages, and other sources). 2. **CHOOSE** an activity from this guide (or from activities you brainstorm to accompany this chapter). Complete a short **SUMMARY** page which includes the goal of the activity, what you learned from participating in it, and the rationale for including this activity product in your portfolio.*	1. Work in groups according to your area of teaching interest to **CREATE A WRITTEN PROFILE** of an effective teacher (in general terms). Support the profile with citations from your course text or other appropriate sources. **PRESENT** your profile to the class and request their feedback. **MAKE CHANGES** you feel are warranted.	1. Work as a class to **WRITE A SUMMARY** of important aspects of this chapter for quick reference in the future. You may want each class member to review a particular page or chapter section and write a one-sentence summary. **COMBINE** each sentence summary (in order), **DUPLICATE,** and **SHARE** with class members.*

*This suggestion may be implemented with individuals, pairs, small groups, or the whole class and can be used for any chapter.

CHILDREN'S LITERATURE CONNECTION

Bourgeois, P., & Clark, B. (1995). *Franklin goes to school.* New York: Scholastic.
   On the first day of school, Franklin's jitters turn to excitement at the hand of a wise and gentle teacher.
Brown, M. (1976). *Arthur's nose.* Boston: Little, Brown.
   There's much more to Arthur than his physical appearance, as is true with all students.
Houston, G. (1992). My Great-Aunt Arizona. New York: HarperCollins.
   An Appalachian girl grows up to be a teacher.

Martin, B., Jr., & Archambault, J. (1966, 1987). *Knots on a counting rope.* New York: Trumpet Club.

Grandfather is a wise teacher, understanding his grandson's need for an oral heritage and faith in himself. How can we be like Grandfather in our approaches to teaching?

Prelutsky, J. (1983). *The Random House book of poetry for children.* New York: Random House.

Includes a wide variety of tried and true children pleasers. "Rules" poem by Karla Kuskin appears on p. 137.

Slate, J. (1996). *Miss Bindergarten gets ready for kindergarten.* New York: Scholastic.

Alphabetical cast of kindergartners prepare for school while their teacher readies the classroom. Good for sparking discussion about what any teacher should prepare and how one selects the most important tasks for the school year.

Thaler, M. (1994). *The gym teacher from the Black Lagoon.* New York: Scholastic.

Students fear the new gym teacher, as his reputation precedes him. Can spark discussion about teacher reputations and how "mean" teachers often turn out to be those we come to love/respect most.

Van Laan, N. (1990). *Possum come a-knockin'.* New York: Alfred A. Knopf.

The rhythmic language in this delightful story offers a chance to view diverse communities and home life experiences in a rich way. Can also suggest that coming to know our students may be much like spotting a possum at the door: We must REALLY look to know and understand what we see.

SUGGESTED READINGS

[2]Baumann, J., & Johnson, D. (1984). *Reading instruction and the beginning teacher: A practical guide.* Minneapolis, MN: Burgess.

This book offers instructions for completing semantic mapping and semantic feature analysis along with numerous examples.

Bolin, F. (1988). Helping student teachers think about teaching. *Journal of Teacher Education, 39*(2), 48–54.

The author describes how student teachers develop a concept of teaching and think about their role as teachers. Through a case study of one preservice teacher's journal entries and interviews with a university supervisor, the author describes stages of development and the role of self-awareness and reflection in becoming an effective teacher.

Borich, G. (1995). *Becoming a teacher: An inquiring dialogue for the beginning teacher.* Bristol, PA: Falmer.

A set of 13 conversations between a young journalist, school principal, and teachers describing an effective school and effective teaching. Through conversational dialogue, the author identifies and illustrates practical ways schools and teachers become effective.

Brophy, J. (2001). *Teaching.* International Academy of Education, International Bureau of Education, United Nations Education, Social and Cultural Organization (UNESCO). Geneva, Switzerland. [On-line], Available: www.ibe.unesco.org.

This booklet is a practical synthesis of principles of effective teaching that have emerged from research in classrooms with which every teacher should be aware.

Cruickshank, D. (1990). *Research that informs teachers and teacher education.* Bloomington, IN: Phi Delta Kappa.

This summary of research identifies the most studied and talked-about characteristics of effective teachers and effective schools. The author provides a helpful summary table at the end that identifies 45 characteristics of effectiveness pertaining to principals, teachers, and classrooms.

[1]Duffelmeyer, F. (1994). Effective Anticipation Guide statements for learning from expository prose. *Journal of Reading, 37*(6), 452–57.

Gives examples of effective and ineffective statements for Anticipation Guides.

Duffy, T. M., & Cunningham, D. J. (1996). Constructivism: Implications for the design and delivery of instruction. In D. J. Jonassen (Ed.), *Handbook of research for educational communications and technology* (pp. 170–198). New York: Macmillan Library Reference.

This chapter provides practical suggestions on how to implement constructivist strategies of teaching in your classroom and how you can function as an able facilitator, coach, and guide for your students' knowledge-building process.

Grossman, P., Wilson, S., & Shulman, L. (1989). Teachers of substance: Subject matter knowledge for teaching. In M. C. Reynolds (Ed.), *Knowledge base for beginning teachers*, New York: Pergamon.

This article explains that one of the first challenges facing beginning teachers is the transformation of their subject matter knowledge into a form that is relevant to students and specific to the task of teaching. The authors identify and illustrate several practical ways teachers can make this transformation.

Miller, M. J. (1992). *Model standards for beginning teacher licensing and development: A resource for state dialogue.* [On-line]. Available: www.ccsso.org/intascst.html.

This article presents the teacher knowledge, dispositions, and performances that a beginning teacher should know and be able to do, known as the Interstate New Teacher Assessment and Support Consortium (INTASC) Standards.

Richardson, V. (1997). Constructivist teaching and teacher education: Theory and practice. In V. Richardson (Ed.), *Constructivist teacher education: Building new understandings* (pp. 3–14). Washington, DC: Falmer Press.

This chapter shows the importance of constructivist teaching strategies that challenge your learners to go beyond the information given to construct their own understandings and meanings of lesson content.

Rosenshine, B., & Stevens, R. (1986). Teaching functions. In M. C. Wittrock (Ed.), *Handbook of research on teaching* (3rd ed., pp. 376–91). Upper Saddle River, NJ: Merrill/Prentice Hall.

This chapter summarizes some of the more generally applicable findings from research on teaching effectiveness, with particular emphasis on those teaching functions related to student achievement.

Ruddell, R. (1995). Those influential literacy teachers: Meaning negotiators and motivation builders. *The Reading Teacher, 48*(6), 454–63.

This article discusses characteristics of influential and motivating educators, and includes 10 instructional insights drawn from such teachers.

Webb, R. (Ed.). (1990). *Practitioner research in the primary school.* New York: Falmer Press.

This book provides models and actual examples of how teachers can become practitioner-researchers in their own classrooms and, in the process, acquire a capacity for directing their own professional development.

Weiss, E. M., & Weiss, S. G. (1998). New directions in teacher evaluation. *ERIC Digest.* Washington, DC: ERIC Clearinghouse on Teaching and Teacher Education. (ERIC Document Reproduction Service No. ED 429 052)

For decades, American teaching reflected a direct instruction model, where teachers were expected to present or "transmit" knowledge to students who were expected to retrieve, store, and return information upon request. This chapter shows how learners do not simply "receive" knowledge; but rather, actively construct knowledge through interacting with the social, cultural, and linguistic context of the classroom.

Vaughn, S., Schumm, J., Niarhos, F., & Gordon, J. (1993). Students' perceptions of two hypothetical teachers' instructional adaptations for low achievers. *Elementary School Journal, 94*(1), 87–102.

A majority of elementary students studied preferred teachers who made adaptations for individual student needs. High achievers were more supportive of teachers who individualized than were low achievers. The authors suggest that perhaps low achievers value inclusion, fitting in, and being "treated the same as the others" over instructional adaptations that single them out as having learning difficulties.

ACTIVE LEARNING

[1]**ANTICIPATION GUIDES** look somewhat like a traditional test, but include two answer columns. One column is labeled "BEFORE READING" and the other is labeled "AFTER READING." Drawing upon prior knowledge and experience, students answer each question before reading a particular text. The questions are generally written in a true/false format, but can also be multiple choice or fill-in. After students answer the questions, they read the text to see how their answers compare to the information in the text. They then return to the questions and answer them a second time (in the "AFTER READING" column), making notes about the changes as desired. Students then discuss the "correct" answers as a group. Note: This activity is especially effective if some of the questions are open-ended enough to encourage broad discussion and sharing of personal opinion and experience.

[2]**THINK, PAIR, SHARE** is a dyad activity in which students work in pairs to complete a learning task. First they consider a question on their own for a minute or two, perhaps jotting notes about their ideas. Then they meet with a partner to compare ideas and come up with a summary of the two ideas (usually within a limited time period, e.g., 2–5 minutes). Each pair then shares its response with another pair of students (making a square) or with the class as a whole. (Note: Shy partners can be involved by asking partners to share ideas they liked, e.g., "Think of something your partner said and share that with the group.")

[3]**MAPPING, WEBBING,** and other **GRAPHIC ORGANIZER TECHNIQUES** are visual illustrations of ideas and concepts, such as flow charts, pie charts, and family trees. The following chart (p. 8) includes four commonly used forms and their purposes (from which you may wish to choose during the course):

Four Types of Graphic Organizers

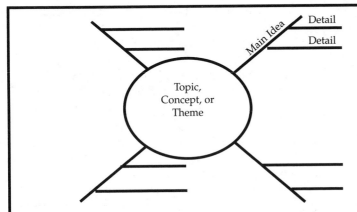

Spider Map: Used to describe a central idea: a thing, process, concept, or proposition with support. Key frame questions: What is the central idea? What are its attributes? What are its functions?

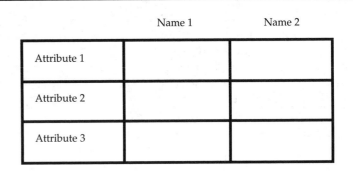

Comparison Matrix: Used to show similarities and differences between two things (e.g., people, places, events, ideas, etc.) Key frame questions: What things are being compared? How are they similar? How are they different?

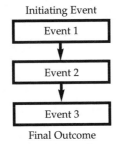

Series of Events Chain: Used to describe the stages of something; the steps in a linear procedure; a sequence of events; or the goals, actions, and outcomes of a historical figure or character in a novel. Key frame questions: What is the object, procedure, or initiating event? What are the stages or steps? How do they lead to one another? What is the final outcome?

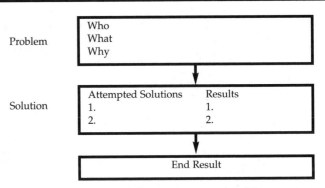

Problem-Solving Frame: Used to represent a problem, attempted solutions, and results. Key frame questions: What was the problem? Who had the problem? Why was it a problem? What attempts were made to solve the problem? Did those attempts succeed?

Source: From "Teaching Students to Construct Graphic Representations," by B. F. Jones, J. Pierce, and B. Hunter, in *Educational Leadership* (pp. 20–25). December 1988/January 1989 vol 6, no. 4. Alexandria, VA: Association for Supervision and Curriculum Development. 1989 ASCD. Reprinted by permission. All rights reserved.

BRIDGES

Chapter 2
Understanding Your Students

Chapter 2	A. *Personal, Dialogue,* *or Buddy Journals*	B. *Self-Directed* *Study Activities*	C. *Cooperative &* *Collaborative Ideas*	D. *Whole* *Class*
Introducing the Content	1. What were you like as a learner? What helped you understand and remember course content? Why do you think that worked? Has your learning pattern changed over the years? In what ways? 2. What concerns you most about becoming a teacher? How do you plan to deal with your concern(s)? 3. **REFLECT** on a time when a teacher failed or succeeded in adapting course content to your background. What happened? Why? How could this experience have been enhanced or avoided?	1. How many "kinds" or "types" of learners do you think there are? What does the term "learning styles" mean to you? **CHOOSE AN ARTICLE OR BOOK** on learning styles or ability grouping/tracking to **READ OR SKIM. REPORT OR SHARE** your findings in some way. 2. **MAKE A LIST** of your perceived strengths and weaknesses in becoming a teacher. How do they relate to those in the text?	1. **DEFINE ABILITY GROUPING** as you understand it. **LIST PROS AND CONS** of ability grouping. How is this related to the concepts of remediation and compensatory teaching approaches discussed in Chapter 2 of your text? 2. What are some educational biases you've experienced or observed? What were the effects of these? How might they be altered? 3. **DISCUSS THE FOLLOWING QUESTIONS** in a small group or with a partner: Can you teach someone to think? How? Why or why not?	1. **CREATE** and **DISPLAY AN OVERHEAD TRANSPARENCY** of students as vessels or blank slates. **DISCUSS** views of teaching and learning over the years and how they have changed to more constructivist notions. 2. **HOLD A DEBATE**[1] on whether you can teach someone to think. Assign teams to support and challenge the idea and plan a structured format for sharing these ideas in class.

Chapter 2 continued	A. Personal, Dialogue, or Buddy Journals	B. Self-Directed Study Activities	C. Cooperative & Collaborative Ideas	D. Whole Class
Assimilating/ Reviewing the Content	4. How might your journal entries for this course relate to the concept of becoming a reflective teacher as discussed in Chapter 1 of your text? How might these ideas relate to your future students? 5. How will your emotional needs be met when you are teaching? What concerns do you have about your own students' needs for emotional support? What can/should you do to support them? Consider a poetic response here, or perhaps a humorous look at ways to survive the stresses of teaching.[2]	3. **WRITE A SHORT PROFILE** of a student you have known (or one you expect to meet). Suggest remediation/ compensatory teaching ideas for adapting to that learner's needs. 4. How does home influence, peer pressure, or television viewing relate to academic achievement? **READ OR SKIM 2–3 SOURCES** dealing with one of these topics. Did your opinion change as a result of your research? **REPORT OR SHARE** your findings in some way.	4. **DISCUSS WITH A PARTNER:** What is intelligence? Can intelligence be "taught"? 5. **THINK OF A VISUAL WAY TO DEPICT THE IDEA** of multiple intelligences. **SHARE** the finished product with the class. 6. Think of a specific curriculum concept and **BRAINSTORM** how that concept might be adapted/expanded to include some of the multiple intelligence ideas. **SHARE** your ideas with the class through a **ROLE PLAY** or other appropriate means.	3. Use practice questions from the chapter to complete a **COVERT RESPONSE TECHNIQUE** (p. 17). **DEBRIEF** on the value of this technique. 4. **BRAINSTORM** influences on learning and categorize. **MAP** (pp. 7–8) and **COMPARE** to the text discussion. 5. Introduce the **CONCEPT MAP** (see p. 16) as an overhead transparency. Trace the ideas with students and discuss how a concept map can enhance understanding.

Chapter 2: Checking Your Understanding

True or False:

1. _____ Social class is a less important factor in educational achievement than is race/ethnicity.

2. _____ Learning styles are stable across children and rarely vary according to race or culture.

3. _____ The practice of ability grouping can actually increase differences in academic performance between groups.

4. _____ Psychologists like Erikson suggest that certain aspects of personality develop or dominate at certain periods in our lives. This idea is important for teachers so they can plan ways to teach other personality traits to students.

5. _____ Teachers must adjust both content and their teaching practices to the average student in the classroom.

6. _____ According to Sternberg, one's ability to adapt to the environment may be a helpful measure of one's intelligence.

7. _____ Social competence is more important in school learning than is IQ.

8. _____ Adaptive teaching means to apply the same instructional strategy to different groups of learners so that all students experience each strategy.

9. _____ Although learning is influenced by several layers or systems, the systems view offers little practical information for day-to-day instructional planning.

10. _____ Some researchers and educators believe that intelligence can be influenced through instruction in specific areas.

11. _____ Compensatory instruction is designed to help a student gain needed information or skills in order to benefit from planned instruction.

12. _____ According to environmentalist thinking, the effect of one's home environment upon one's IQ is at least as important as heredity.

13. _____ Students from low SES (socioeconomic status) homes have generally had a good deal of experience with the same kinds of activities that go on at school.

14. _____ Students need successful horizontal relationships so they can compare themselves with others.

15. _____ It is more important to know a student's general ability and intelligence rather than his or her specific aptitudes.

16. _____ All anxiety interferes with learning.

17. _____ Some researchers claim that humans have specialized abilities which influence general performance.

1. F	2. F	3. T	4. F	5. F	6. T	7. T	8. F
9. F	10. T	11. T	12. T	13. F	14. F	15. F	16. F	17. T

Chapter 2: Performance Assessment Ideas		
Individual	*Small Group*	*Whole Class*
1. **LIST AND EXPLAIN 2–3** alternatives to ability grouping for meeting special needs of students. How or why are these alternatives desirable? 2. **CREATE A CONCEPT MAP** (like the one on p. 16) for another course assignment and use it for studying the content. Write a short **SUMMARY** of how the map helped you (or failed to help you) in your study. Include a copy of the map with your summary.	1. **REFLECT** on how your group work in this course has been similar to or different from ability grouping contexts. **WRITE** your ideas in the form of a short essay, a persuasive poem, or other communicative device (see p. 32 for a list of ideas).*	1. Obtain a description of students' abilities in a particular subject and grade from a teacher currently teaching. As a class, **BRAINSTORM** suggestions for grouping strategies this teacher might use to meet the learning needs of the students. **WRITE** up your final ideas and submit to the teacher. (You may want to break into small groups for the writing portion of this experience.) 2. Work in small groups to **GENERATE** scenarios about which teachers may feel concern (e.g., discipline issues, teaching difficulties). It is best if the scenarios are drawn from actual events and experiences. **COPY** and **SHARE** the scenarios. Hold a class **DISCUSSION** regarding ways to solve each of the scenario problems. At its conclusion, **ASK** class members to **EVALUATE** the usefulness of the activity and **WRITE** about how it affected their professional growth and understanding.

*Many assessment ideas will apply across chapters, so you may also want to review previous (and forthcoming) assessment ideas.

CHILDREN'S LITERATURE CONNECTION

Cohen, M. (1967). *Will I have a friend?* New York: Scholastic.

Jim's concern on his first day of school about whether he'll have a friend can foster class discussion about student relationships in class.

Diakité, B. W. (1997). *The hunterman and the crocodile.* New York: Scholastic.

Donso learns a lesson from the animals and plants that helps him see his place in the world. Could spark discussion about social priorities and how classrooms are marked by give and take.

Geisel, T. S. (Dr. Seuss). (1979). *Oh say can you say?* New York: Random House.

This book of extended tongue twisters provides an entertaining look at the power and challenge of language—offering an interesting introduction to thinking about the different discourse communities and language abilities among the students in our classrooms.

Gwynne, F. (1976). *A chocolate moose for dinner.* New York: Trumpet Club.

Highlights how confusing homonyms and idioms in English can be. May provide some insight for difficulties encountered by English language learners in our classrooms.

Hoffman, M. (1991). *Amazing Grace.* New York: Dial Books for Young Readers.

Grace's home support is a key to her success at school.

Johnson, A. (1989). *Tell me a story, mama.* New York: Trumpet Club.

The author comes from a rich oral tradition—we can tap the backgrounds of our students if we learn about them.

Jonas, A. (1983). *Round trip.* New York: Greenwillow.

Depending on how you view them, the same pictures tell two stories. This is much like viewing our students through different frames or perspectives.

Lionnie, L. (1963). *Swimmy.* New York: Random House.

Just as the fish discover, each of us has an important role to play within the group.

Lobel, A. (1982). *Ming Lo moves the mountain.* New York: Scholastic.

Just as Ming Lo achieves his goals step by step, so teachers achieve planning skill and instructional success in a step-by-step manner.

Monson, A. M. (1997). *Wanted: Best friend.* New York: Scholastic.

Just like our students, Cat learns how friendship really works—through negotiation and experiences with others.

Paulson, T. (1990). *The beanstalk incident.* New York: Carol Publishing Group.

Twist on Jack and the Beanstalk which suggests there is more than one view of an event.

Scieszka, J. (1989). *The true story of the 3 little pigs!* New York: Viking.

An important part of learning that any event is viewed from multiple perspectives, just as in this story.

Shorto, Russell. (1990). *Cinderella: The untold story.* New York: Carol Publishing Group.

Cinderella's sister has a slightly different view of the well-known story. Just as she offers a different perspective, it can be helpful to view our curriculum goals and approaches from more than one perspective, since choosing what to emphasize also means choosing things to overlook or deemphasize.

Trivizas, E., & Oxenbury, H. (1993). *The three little wolves and the big bad pig.* New York: Scholastic.

This twist on a well-known fairy tale can open up discussion on perspective and knowing our students. In contrast to the usual stereotype of wolves as the bad guys, the wolves in this story are gentle—suggesting the possibility for teachers to view students with new lenses.

Waber, B. (1966). *You look ridiculous.* Boston: Houghton Mifflin.

A hippo discovers she can't be all things to all people, just as we must discover as teachers.

Zolotow, Charlotte. (1989). *Someday.* New York: HarperTrophy.

Ellen dreams of all the wonderful things that will happen "someday"—a little like the big teaching goals and plans we must sometimes downsize to make attainable.

SUGGESTED READINGS

Bintz, W. P. (1995). Reflections on teaching in multicultural settings. *The Social Studies, 86*(1), 39–42.
  Suggests that education models should be based on the need for diversity rather than similarity among students.
Bullock, J. (1993, November). Shy kids: Don't shy away. *Education Digest, 57–8.*
  Suggests that most "shy" children are not at-risk and will overcome the shyness over time.
Burnette, J. (1999). Critical behaviors and strategies for teaching culturally diverse students. *ERIC/OSEP Digest E 584.* Arlington, VA: ERIC
  Clearinghouse on Disabilities and Gifted Education. (ERIC Document Reproduction Service No. ED 435 147)
  The author explains why culturally sensitive teachers consider students' cultures and language skills when planning learning objectives and activities and how to develop lesson objectives that add to their students' affective and personal development.
[1]Butz, C. S. (1995). Great debate! *The Reading Teacher, 48*(7), 618–9.
  Describes her own experience in setting up a third grade debate which can be adapted to many other settings.
Cheng, L. (1996, October). Enhancing communication: Toward optimal language learning for limited English proficient students. *Language, Speech and Hearing Services in Schools, 28*(2), 347–54.
  This author describes a number of important differences among students including: linguistic distance between the native language and English, students' varying levels of proficiency in their native language, students' past experiences with English, and their desire to learn English that must be taken into consideration when planning lessons for culturally diverse learners.
Davern, L. (1996, April). Listening to parents of children with disabilities. *Educational Leadership, 61–3.*
  Offers teachers some concrete ideas for working with disabled students and their families.
Delgado-Gaitan, C. (1991). Involving parents in the schools: A process of empowerment. *American Educational Research Journal, 100*(1), 20–46.
  A report of research involving several minority communities in which strategies were successful in getting parents involved in their neighborhood school.
Diller, D. (1999). Opening the dialogue: Using culture as a tool in teaching young African American children. *The Reading Teacher, 52*(8), 820–8.
  The author explains how teachers' own experiences can sometimes act as blinders, and may actually exclude them from discovering important insights that would make their teaching more effective with students from other cultures.
Gardner, H. (1999). Are there additional intelligences? The case for naturalist, spiritual, and existential intelligences. In J. Kane (Ed.), *Education, information and transformation* (pp. 111–31). Upper Saddle River, NJ: Prentice Hall.
  One way to plan for instructional variety is to consider Gardner's concept of multiple intelligences—and ask students to respond to various tasks using different intelligences.
Griggs, S., & Dunn, R. (1996). Hispanic American students and learning style. *ERIC Digest.* Washington, DC: Office of Educational Research and
  Improvement & U.S. Department of Education. (ERIC Document Reproduction Service No. ED 393 607)
  These authors present convincing arguments that different cultures react differently to the nonverbal and verbal behavioral management techniques of proximity control, eye contact, warnings, and classroom arrangement. Furthermore, these authors cite numerous examples of how teachers from one culture interpret behaviors of children differently than teachers from another culture.
Harter, S. (1990). Processes underlying adolescent self-concept formation. In R. Montemajor, G. R. Adams, & T. P. Gullota (Eds.), *From childhood to adolescence: A transitional period?* (pp. 205–39). Newbury Park, CA: Sage.
  This chapter reviews how one acquires self-concept during the critical adolescent years and the many sources of influence within a school that can shape its development.

Hartup, W. (1989). Social relationships and their developmental significance. *American Psychologist, 44,* 120–6.
Description of the role of horizontal and vertical friendships and how they can influence the social-emotional development of the school child.

Hill, H. (1989). *Effective strategies for teaching minority students.* Bloomington, IN: National Educational Service.
A guide to successfully teaching minority youth and developing cultural sensitivity that promotes learning and achievement.

Huber, T. (1992). Culturally responsible pedagogy: "The case of Josefina Guzman." *Teaching Education, 5*(1), 123–31.
Describes how one teacher comes to know and meet her students' needs.

Irvine, J., & York, D. (2001). Learning Styles and Culturally Diverse Students: A Literature Review. In J. Banks & C. Banks (Eds.), *Handbook of research on multicultural education* (pp. 484–97). San Francisco: Jossey-Bass.
These authors provide examples and research that support how your students' learning styles can determine how much they learn and, most importantly, how your teaching strategies can maximize what is learned.

Jackson, F. R. (1993/1994). Seven strategies to support a culturally responsive pedagogy. *Journal of Reading, 37*(4), 298–303.
Offers seven areas for teachers to consider in becoming more culturally sensitive.

Kreidler, W. J. (1995, January/February). Say good-bye to bias. *Instructor,* 28.
Describes several activities to embrace diversity within the classroom.

Lockwood, A. T., & Secada, W. G. (1999, January). *Transforming education for Hispanic youth: Exemplary practices, programs, and schools. NCBE Resource Collection Series, No. 12.* Washington, DC: National Clearinghouse for Bilingual Education.
Lockwood and Secada summarize the findings of the national Hispanic Dropout Project (HDP) and cite specific school programs and instructional strategies that support not only the education of Hispanic students, but all students.

Magliocca, L. A., & Robinson, N. M. (1991). The "I Can" strategy for promoting self-confidence. *Teaching Exceptional Children, 23*(2), 30–3.
The authors describe the "I Can" strategy, based on methods used by general education master teachers with a history of success in working with at-risk students. Specific strategies are grouped under the following student skill areas: reading; responding to questions; taking risks in learning; and being a group member. Students may want to refer back to this article when they read Chapters 7, 9–11 in the text.

Marshall, P. L. (1995, March). Misconceiving multicultural education. *Education Digest,* 57–60.
Challenges four common misconceptions about multicultural education.

[2]McVeigh-Schultz, J. (1995). Poetry and assessment. *Language Arts 72*(1), 39–41.
Suggests that having students create poetry can provide a fresh assessment tool.

Miller, H. M. (2000). Teaching and learning about cultural diversity: All of us together have a story to tell. *The Reading Teacher, 53*(6), 666–7.
This author explains how you can acquire the concept of "intercultural competence"—or the ability to interact smoothly and effectively with members of various cultures.

Purcell-Gates, V., L'Allier, S., & Smith, D. (1995). Literacy at the Harts' and the Larsons': Diversity among poor, inner city families. *The Reading Teacher, 48*(7), 572–8.
Notes the wide variation in how family members use print in the home.

Walqui, A. (2000). *Access and engagement: Program design and instructional approaches for immigrant students in secondary school. (Topics in Immigrant Education 4, Language in Education: Theory and Practice 94),* Washington, DC: Center for Applied Linguistics.
Walqui suggests that although some students may have been socialized to recitation and lecture formats, more active instructional approaches encourage English Language Learners to engage in deeper language processing and conceptual learning.

Concept Map: Chapter 2

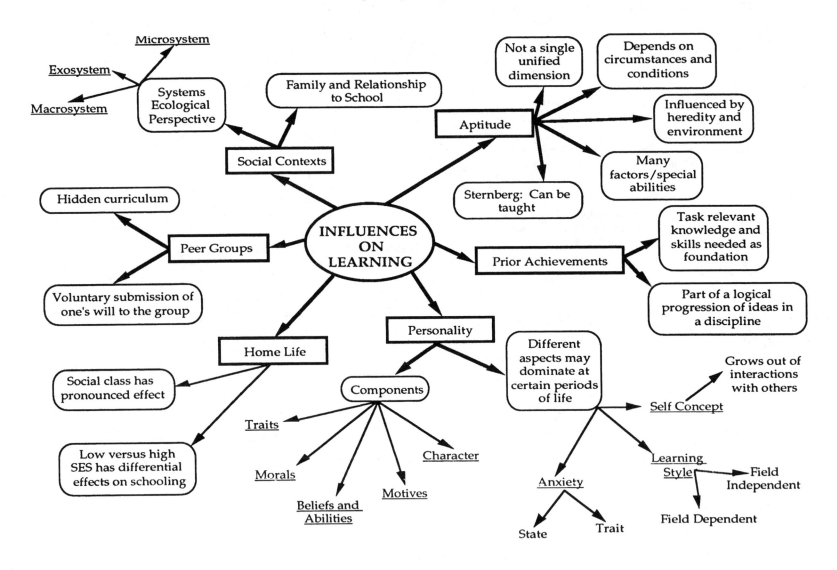

ACTIVE LEARNING

In the **COVERT RESPONSE TECHNIQUE** the teacher poses a question and asks students to respond by holding up some sort of private signal (thumbs up, "yes" or "no" cards, etc.) that only the teacher can see. In this way, students demonstrate their understanding of a concept in a nonevaluative, risk-free environment. Seeing all the responses allows the teacher to immediately assess student understanding and determine the next instructional step.

BRIDGES

KNOWLEDGE

Chapter 3
Goals and Objectives

ACTIVITY

Chapter 3	A. *Personal, Dialogue, or Buddy Journals*	B. *Self-Directed Study Activities*	C. *Cooperative & Collaborative Ideas*	D. *Whole Class*
Introducing the Content	1. What comes to your mind when you think of goals and plans? Are these useful to you in your personal growth? How might your knowledge and experience with goals and plans enhance/ inhibit your work as a teacher seeking to organize curriculum? 2. **COMPARE** the concept of a "thinking" curriculum (in your text) with your own school experiences.	1. **REFLECT** on the author's claim that behavioral objectives need a learning outcome, conditions, and criterion levels to be effective. Is this so? Why or why not? 2. **SELECT** a children's book* from those listed on pp. 62–64. **CREATE AN ACTIVITY** that young students could do to better understand or recall the book's main concept(s).	1. In groups, **DISCUSS** the following question: What is it that behavioral objectives do for teachers? 2. In groups, **BRAIN-STORM** some community values common to a specific setting. How might these influence teaching goals and plans? How can a teacher become aware of these if s/he begins teaching in an unfamiliar setting?	1. **DISPLAY A VISUAL** of Escher's staircase or other optical illusion where the eye seems to keep moving yet fails to progress. Discuss how well-conceived and well-written behavioral objectives help teachers achieve more than just an "illusion" of progress. 2. Complete a **K-W-L** activity (p. 24)[1] before reading or discussing the chapter:

*Books are marked with an asterisk.

Chapter 3 continued	A. Personal, Dialogue, or Buddy Journals	B. Self-Directed Study Activities	C. Cooperative & Collaborative Ideas	D. Whole Class
Assimilating/ Reviewing the Content	3. How do you feel about a "standard" or "set" curriculum as opposed to a more flexible, open approach? What advantages or disadvantages do you see in outlining curriculum carefully and in detail? 4. How can/should teachers set criterion levels for behavioral objectives? How could/should criterion levels change over time?	**PRESENT** your plans to your classmates and ask them to brainstorm which cognitive, affective, and psychomotor levels your activity encompasses. 3. **WRITE** 2–3 intentionally vague or "bad" behavioral objectives for Activity 3-C-5.	3. **BRAINSTORM** related terms for the words "learning outcomes" "conditions," and "criterion levels." **MAP** the terms and ideas (pp. 7–8) for each of the three words. Talk about why good behavioral objectives must include all three ideas. 4. **MAP** Chapter 3 or a key part of the chapter (pp. 7–8). Make your map into a recipe or graphic of some sort and **EXPLAIN** it to the class. 5. Work in pairs with poorly written behavioral objectives to **CORRECT** and **SHARE** them (can be chosen from those created in Activity 4-B-3). Use the **BEHAVIORAL OBJECTIVE PLANNING SHEET** (p. 25) to help you improve the objectives.	What do we know about goals and plans for teaching? What do we want to know? 3. **BRAINSTORM** the meaning of the term "curriculum." Where does curriculum come from and what should be taught? How should it be taught (planning)? What is meant by "hidden curriculum"? 4. **DISCUSS** the **BEHAVIORAL OBJECTIVE PLANNING SHEET** (p. 25) with the class and describe the importance of the three areas in writing useful behavioral objectives.

Chapter 3: Checking Your Understanding

Match the following terms with your own definitions or summary statements taken from the text:

aims	thinking curriculum	psychomotor	behavioral objectives
goals	cognitive	criterion levels	learning outcomes
objectives	affective	learning activity	conditions
authentic assessment	indirect assessment	performance-based assessment	

True or False:

1. _____ All objectives require a single correct response.
2. _____ Generally, those behavioral objectives requiring higher level cognitive, affective, and psychomotors skill will be more authentic.
3. _____ Behaviors of less complexity are always easier to teach than those at higher levels.
4. _____ The purpose of the content-by-behavior blueprint is to help teachers discover behaviors they may have failed to include in their lesson plans.
5. _____ A good reason for stating the level of performance in a behavioral objective is to provide some way to determine whether the behavior has been obtained.
6. _____ An authentic objective is one which reflects behaviors most like those needed for living in the "real" world.

1. F   2. T   3. F   4. T   5. T   6. T

Chapter 3: Performance Assessment Ideas		
Individual	*Small Group*	*Whole Class*
1. Obtain a copy of the curriculum guide for a grade/setting in which you would like to teach. **REVIEW** its contents and **WRITE A REACTION** to it. What do you see as strengths? Weaknesses? What ideas for teaching units come to your mind? 2. **READ** the article by Cornbleth[2] and **RESPOND** to her points about influences on curriculum. What groups or viewpoints appear most strongly represented in the curriculum taught in the schools in your area? How do you feel about this?	1. Obtain a copy of a curriculum guide for a specific subject area or grade level you'd like to teach. Meet with a small group of others with similar interests and **CRITIQUE THE GUIDE'S CONTENTS.** What important ideas/connections do you see in the guide? What might you alter? Why? Do you see evidence of a "thinking curriculum" emphasis in the guide? 2. Work in groups to **REVISE** the **BEHAVIORAL OBJECTIVE PLANNING SHEET** (p. 25) in some way to make it more useful for you. **SHARE** your revisions with class members, and support your changes from appropriate sources.	1. Work in small groups to **WRITE 1–2** behavioral objectives that could apply to the course. **COPY** and **SHARE** the objectives. Hold a class **DISCUSSION** to improve the clarity of several of the written objectives. 2. **BRAINSTORM** some things you have learned in this course. Individually or in small groups, divide this list and create behavioral objectives that could have supported this learning. Share your ideas with class members and make appropriate changes.

*Remember to review assessment suggestions for all other chapters—many ideas will apply throughout the course.

CHILDREN'S LITERATURE CONNECTION

Geisel, T. (Dr. Seuss). *Oh, the places you'll go!* New York: Random House.
  Motivational take on one's ability to succeed.
Tworkov, J. (1951). *The camel who took a walk.* New York: Trumpet Club.
  Sometimes plans don't work, as the animals in this story discover.

SUGGESTED READINGS

[2]Cornbleth, C. (1995). Controlling curriculum knowledge: Multicultural politics and policymaking. *Journal of Curriculum Studies, 27*(2), 165–85.
> *Describes some of the arguments in New York about a multicultural social studies curriculum. Observes that there are numerous influences on what is chosen as approved curriculum.*

Epstein, J. (1997/1998). Cognitive development in an integrated mathematics and science program. *Journal of College Science Teaching, 27*(3), 194–201.
> *Although a remedial college course is described, several points worthy of consideration by teachers in other settings are made.*

Fielding, L. G., & Pearson, P. D. (1994). Reading comprehension: What works. *Educational Leadership, 51*(5), 62–8.
> *The authors summarize several decades of reading research and arrive at four characteristics of a successful reading instruction program: 1) ample time for actual text reading; 2) teacher-directed comprehension strategy instruction; 3) opportunities for peer and collaborative learning; and 4) time for discussing what has been read.*

Gronlund, N. (1995). *How to write and use instructional objectives* (5th ed.). Upper Saddle River, NJ: Merrill/Prentice Hall.
> *This is a practical text written especially for teachers on how objectives can be used for effective teaching across different grades and content areas.*

Kennedy, M. (Ed.). (1991). *Teaching academic subjects to diverse learners.* New York: Teachers College Press.
> *This book contains chapters by subject area specialists in the areas of science and mathematics. The various authors discuss effective teaching methods specific to these disciplines. They also address the challenges that classes of diverse learners present to teachers.*

Kincade, L. (1996). Resurrecting history in the high school classroom. *Social Studies Review, 35*(3), 10–1.
> *A high school teacher describes how she makes history come alive for her students.*

Marzano, R. J. (1996). Eight questions about implementing standards-based education. *ERIC/AE Digest Series.* Washington, DC: ERIC Clearinghouse on Teaching and Teacher Education. (ERIC Document Reproduction Service No. ED 410 230)
> *During the past decade, there have been a number of national and state standards efforts, such as those by the National Council of Teacher of Mathematics (NCTM), the International Reading Association (IRA), and others, which have sought to define the knowledge and performance required of students or teachers in particular subject areas. This author reviews their similarities and differences as well as their weaknesses and strengths.*

Monson, R. J., & Monson, M. P. (1994). Literacy as inquiry: An interview with Jerome C. Harste. *The Reading Teacher, 47*(7), 518–21.
> *Harste, a well-known reading educator, suggests that the curriculum of the future can and should be based on student-generated inquiry.*

National Council for the Social Studies. (1994). *Expectations of excellence: Curriculum standards for social studies.* Washington, DC: National Council for the Social Studies.

National Council of Teachers of English. (1996). *Standards for the English language arts.* Urbana, IL: National Council of Teachers of English and International Reading Association.

National Council of Teachers of Mathematics. (1995). *Assessment standards for school mathematics,* Reston, VA: National Council of Teachers of Mathematics.

National Research Council. (1996). *National science education standards 1995.* Washington, DC: National Academy Press.
> *These reports provide the essential curriculum standards for the teaching of social studies, English and language arts, mathematics, and science with which teachers of any one or all of these curriculum areas should be aware.*

Pasch, M., Sparks-Langer, G., Gardner, T. G., Starko, A. J., & Moody, C. D. (1991). *Teaching as decision-making: Instructional practices for the classroom teacher.* New York: Longman.
This text contains numerous practical exercises to help teachers with instructional planning. It emphasizes the day-to-day decisions teachers must make when choosing goals, objectives, and strategies for learners.

Schweinhart, L. J., & Weikart, D. P. (1998). Why curriculum matters in early childhood education. *Educational Leadership, 66*(6), 57–61.
This article discusses the long-term effects of curriculum choices on preschool children. It may raise some interesting discussion regarding whether a teacher's curriculum decisions affect more than the current year of the students' lives and in what ways.

Shanks, J. (1994). Students' reactions to a standardized curriculum: A case study. *Journal of Curriculum and Supervision, 10*(1), 43–59.
Describes the change in viewpoint among teachers and students when Burr Oaks Elementary adopted a standardized, textbook-based curriculum. Definitions of learning narrowed and teachers felt hampered in meeting students' individual needs.

[1]Sippola, A. E. (1995). K-W-L-S. *The Reading Teacher, 48*(6), 542–3.
Suggests an additional column on the traditional K-W-L chart for "What I still need to learn."

ACTIVE LEARNING

K-W-L is an instructional strategy where the teacher uses brainstorming and direct questioning with the whole class to determine what they **KNOW (K)** about the content from prior instruction and personal experiences. Ask students what they already know about the topic. List all ideas the students generate (correct or incorrect). Note disagreements and questions in the center column as questions to be answered and things they **WANT (W)** to learn. Students read to answer their question, jotting down information and new questions that arise. (You may even have students read to answer their own personal questions they write.) After reading, students articulate what they have **LEARNED (L)** and what they still need to learn. Remaining questions may be used for further research and inquiry.

Ogel, D. (1986). K-W-L: A teaching model that develops active reading of expository text. *The Reading Teacher, 39,* 564–71.

K-W-L Chart

What We KNOW (K)	What We WANT to Find Out (W)	What We LEARNED (L)

Behavioral Objective Planning Sheet: Chapter 3

Characterization	Behavior is consistent with one's values. Avoid, display, exhibit, internalize, manage, require, resist, resolve, revise
Organization	Hold a commitment to a set of values. Form a reason why one values certain things and not others, makes appropriate choices between things that are and are not valued. Abstract, balance, compare, decide, define, formulate, select, systematize, theorize
Valuing	Display behavior consistent with a single belief or attitude in situations where one is neither forced nor asked to comply. Demonstrate a preference or display a high degree of certainty and conviction. Act, argue, convince, debate, display, express, help, organize, prefer
Responding	Comply with given expectations by attending or reacting to certain stimuli. Obey, participate, respond willingly when asked or directed to do something. Applaud, comply, discuss, follow, obey, participate, play, practice, volunteer
Receiving	Be aware of, or passively attend to certain phenomena and stimuli. Listen, be attentive. Attend, beware, control, discern, hear, listen, look, notice, share

AFFECTIVE

Naturalization	Behavior is performed with the least expenditure of energy and becomes routine, automatic, spontaneous, and occurs at a high level of proficiency. Automatically, effortlessly, naturally, professionally, routinely, spontaneously, with ease, with perfection, with poise
Articulation	Display coordination of a series of related acts by establishing the appropriate sequence and performing the acts accurately, with control as well as with speed and timing. Confidence, coordination, harmony, integration, proportion, smoothness, speed, stability, timing
Precision	Perform an action independent of either a visual model or a written set of directions. Reproduce the action with control and reduce errors to a minimum. Accurately, errorlessly, independently, proficiently, with control, with balance
Manipulation	Perform selected actions from written or verbal directions without the aid of a visual model or direct observations. Same active verbs as "Imitation" level, but performed from spoken or written (rather than visual) instructions.
Imitation	Be exposed to an observable action and overtly imitate it, even at a crude and imperfect level. Align, balance, follow, grasp, hold, place, repeat, rest (on), step (here)

PSYCHOMOTOR

Evaluation	Form judgments and make decisions about the value of methods, ideas, people, or products that have a specific purpose. State the basis for these judgments. Appraise, compare, contrast, defend, judge, justify, support, validate
Synthesis	Produce something unique or original. Solve some unfamiliar problem in a unique way or combine parts to form a unique or novel solution. Categorize, compile, compose, create, design, devise, formulate, predict, produce
Analysis	Identify logical errors (contradiction, erroneous inference) or differentiate among facts, opinions, assumptions, hypotheses, and conclusions. Draw relationships among ideas and compare and contrast. Break down, deduce, diagram, differentiate, distinguish, illustrate, infer, outline, point out, relate, separate out, subdivide
Application	Use previously acquired information in a setting other than the one in which it was learned. Change, compute, demonstrate, develop, modify, operate, organize, prepare, relate, solve, transfer, use
Comprehension	Change the form of a communication; translate; restate what has been read; see connections or relationships among parts of a communication; draw conclusions or see consequences from its information. Convert, defend, discriminate, distinguish, estimate, explain, extend, generalize, infer, paraphrase, predict, summarize
Knowledge	Remember or recall information such as facts, terminology, problem-solving strategies and rules. Define, describe, identify, label, list, match, name, outline, recall, recite, select, state

COGNITIVE

BRIDGES

Chapter 4
Unit and Lesson Planning

KNOWLEDGE ———————— ACTIVITY

Chapter 4	A. *Personal, Dialogue, or Buddy Journals*	B. *Self-Directed Study Activities*	C. *Cooperative & Collaborative Ideas*	D. *Whole Class*
Introducing the Content	1. Do you **RECALL** a unit of study you liked/ disliked? What was your learning like? What do you remember? Was it more/less memorable than other school experiences? Why? 2. What gets your attention in class? What makes your attention drift off? What has happened/what do you mean when you say you have "learned" something? How do you learn best? What makes it hard for you to learn something?	1. **FIND A PUBLISHED UNIT OF STUDY** for the area in which you'd like to teach. **ANALYZE** it for attention-getting potential. What changes might you make to enhance its appeal to students? 2. **REVIEW** a unit you've created in the past or one in which you've participated. What attention-getters and other useful devices were employed? What might have enhanced the unit?	1. **DISCUSS IN PAIRS:** What is the most effective way to learn something new? What is the most effective way to **TEACH** something new? Are these the same or different? Why? 2. **BRAINSTORM** several attention-getters for general or specific units of study. Why would each of these be effective?	1. Place ingredients for a cake on the table. **DISCUSS** the idea that in combining ingredients to make a cake, the whole will actually be greater than the sum of the parts. **DRAW THE PARALLEL** that in good unit plans, the result of the whole unit of study is greater than the sum of the separate lessons. If desired, actually **MAKE THE CAKE** and enjoy it as a treat to make the point even more salient!

Chapter 4 continued	A. Personal, Dialogue, or Buddy Journals	B. Self-Directed Study Activities	C. Cooperative & Collaborative Ideas	D. Whole Class
Assimilating/ Reviewing the Content	3. Are there universals that help everyone learn? If you think so, what are some of these? 4. The acronym "K.I.S.S." sometimes stands for "Keep it simple, stupid." How might this mnemonic be helpful when considering linking lessons to a larger unit plan? 5. Your author suggests that visual devices can be effective for organizing thinking. Have you experienced the use of visual devices recently? How were they helpful/not helpful to you? 6. Do you **RECALL** experiences with peer or cross-age tutoring? What occurred? What would you change?	3. **RESPOND** to the idea that learning must be accompanied by a change in behavior. Do you agree or disagree? Why? 4. **CREATE A VISUAL DEVICE** for this chapter (or for a related reading) which will help you remember key concepts or help you teach with them (pp. 7–8). Share your ideas if you desire. 5. **OBSERVE** a teacher in a setting where you would like to teach. **LIST** the schedule s/he follows (including transitions and breaks). If possible, **TALK** to the teacher and find out how the schedule deviated from her/his plan; and how s/he schedules the day, month, year, etc. **ASK** if there are particular routines s/he has found helpful over the years.	3. **THINK OF A SKILL** you could teach. **PLAN** a fifteen-minute lesson and come prepared next time to **TEACH** it to a partner or small group. **DEBRIEF** on your techniques. **INCLUDE A VISUAL DEVICE** to aid your learners. 4. **WORK IN PAIRS** to **COMPLETE A LESSON PLAN** using the **GAGNÉ** form (pp. 33–34). Consider including some of the ideas from the **ACTIVE LEARNING** section of this chapter to add variety to your plan (p. 32). 5. **PERUSE** a published unit of study in an area of teaching interest. **COMPARE** the format to the concepts in the Gagné plan (pp. 33–34). What do you think?	2. **BRAINSTORM** with the group what it means to "learn" something. How do you know it's been learned? 3. Display a cartoon on an overhead transparency, such as two dogs looking at a forest while one laments, "So many trees, so little time." Thus it is with teaching: if we try to accomplish each objective separately, we can be overwhelmed and ineffective. Objectives can and must be combined—for our own sanity and to enhance connections students make. 4. As a class, **READ** the *Reading Teacher* article[1] on group sizes and **DISCUSS** the ideas of planning for different groups. These group sizes should be considered in lesson planning.

Chapter 4: Checking Your Understanding

True or False:

1. _____ Curriculum guides usually specify clearly the level of behavioral complexity students are expected to attain in a particular grade or course.

2. _____ Adopted texts and other materials fail to sequence content according to the needs of specific learners.

3. _____ Unit plans precede lesson plans so you know where you're trying to take your students.

4. _____ Computer-assisted instruction is most effective for teaching new material to under-prepared students.

5. _____ Beginning teachers generally include too much new material in their lessons.

6. _____ It is best to plan evaluative activities like tests and research papers near the middle of a unit so students can see what else they need to learn before the unit ends.

7. _____ It is generally recommended that cross-age tutors be separated from their tutees by 3–4 grade levels.

8. _____ A true system does not exist unless the relationships among parts of the system or unit are planned to connect and build over time.

9. _____ Once determined, criterion levels of behavioral objectives should not be altered.

10. _____ Teachers should organize and sequence curriculum content according to the needs of their students.

11. _____ Teachers should depend primarily upon curriculum guides and textbooks to determine how much content to include in each lesson of a unit.

Matching:

a. programmed instruction
b. tacit knowledge
c. vertical unit planning
d. task ability grouping
e. system perspective
f. learning centers
g. lateral unit planning

12. _____ insight gained through everyday experiences which can guide teaching decisions

13. _____ seeing lessons as part of a larger system of interrelated learning

14. _____ content to be taught is sequenced hierarchically or in steps

15. _____ content is integrated across disciplines to convey relationships in a systematic way

16. _____ students are grouped for a specified period of time by skills needed

17. _____ students work at real-world problem solving by completing particular tasks

18. _____ written instructional materials with which students work individually at their own pace

1. F	2. T	3. T	4. F	5. T	6. F	7. F	8. T	9. F	10. T	11. F
12. b	13. e	14. c	15. g	16. d	17. f	18. a				

Chapter 4: Performance Assessment Ideas		
Individual	*Small Group*	*Whole Class*
1. **USE** the systems idea and **MAP** (pp. 7–8) a specific system with which you are familiar—include names of schools, communities, etc. as applicable. How does creating the map affect your view of each of the components of the system and their interrelations? 2. **CONTACT** a local school district and **DETERMINE** the suggested time allocations per subject for a grade level you would like to teach (i.e., 45 minutes daily for mathematics, etc.) **CHART** your findings and **RESPOND** to the suggestions. What would you alter? Why?	1. **WORK** with a small group to **CREATE** some guidelines for peer tutors that a teacher might use to train older students in working with younger peers. You may **CONSULT** appropriate sources (such as your course text and related professional journal articles) for ideas, but be sure and **ACKNOWLEDGE** the sources used in your final guidelines. 2. **READ** the article referenced below[2] and **RESPOND** to the authors' contention that how a teacher translates a curriculum idea into integrated themes is of utmost importance.	1. **OBTAIN** a state or district curriculum guide for a local school. As a group, **REVIEW** the guide for strengths and weaknesses. What recommendations would you make to a state or district curriculum committee for changes to the guide? **SUPPORT** your recommendations with appropriate source material.

CHILDREN'S LITERATURE CONNECTION

Fleischman, Paul. (1988). *Joyful noise*. New York: Trumpet Club.
  This unique book of poetry for two readers gives a different spin to poetry writing and reading. It may give you ideas for other creative ways to use the arts in your units.
Lionni, Leo. (1967). *Frederick*. New York: Alfred A. Knopf.
  The field mice find that Frederick's poetry helps pass the cold winter days and is, in many ways, as helpful as the food gathered. In like manner, the power of interdisciplinary approaches (bringing the arts and other disciplines together) enhances the learning experiences of our students.
Numeroff, L. J. (1991). *If you give a moose a muffin*. New York: HarperCollins.
  Just as one thing leads to another with the moose, so should one lesson lead to the next in your units.
Prelutsky, Jack. (1983). *The Random House book of poetry for children*. New York: Random House.
  Includes a wide variety of tried and true children pleasers.

Prelutsky, Jack. (1984). *The new kid on the block*. New York: Scholastic.
  This collection of poems by a well-known poet can be used to add fun and interest to units of study, or as attention-getters for specific lessons (as discussed in Chapter 4 of your course text).
Wood, A. (1984). *The napping house*. San Diego: Harcourt Brace Jovanovich.
  This addictive story flows from one thing to another, just like a well-planned unit.

SUGGESTED READINGS

Block, J. (1987). Mastery learning models. In M. J. Dunkin (Ed.), *International encyclopedia of teaching and teacher education*. New York: Pergamon.
  An excellent article on how to achieve mastery learning and what this important concept means for effective teaching.
Bonniwell, T., Coburn, D., & McCarter, W. S. (1998). To build a boat. *Educational Leadership, 55*(6), 54–5.
  Students at a Virginia high school integrate history, biology, and English through the Legacy program.
Campbell, J. (1994). Managing the primary curriculum: The issue of time allocation. *Education, 22*(1), 3–13.
  Discusses time allocated to each subject and teachers' views of the adequacy of those allocations.
Cohen, S. (1987). Instructional alignment: Searching for the magic bullet. *Educational Researcher, 16*(8), 16–20.
  This article explains what an effective objective is and the important process of matching learning activities with objectives called "instructional alignment."
Countryman, J. (1933, January). Writing to learn mathematics. *Teaching: K–8,* 51–3.
  Describes a number of strategies for connecting writing and mathematics in meaningful ways which can be applied and adapted across grade levels.
Dunkin, M. J. (1987). Lesson formats. In M. J. Dunkin (Ed.), *International encyclopedia of teaching and teacher education*. New York: Pergamon.
  A sampling of the many varieties of and ways to prepare lesson plans.
Flagg, A. (1995). *Hands-on-minds-on-science: Our bodies, early childhood*. Huntington Beach, CA: Teacher Created Materials, Inc.
  Suggests a guided discovery lesson plan and gives numerous ideas for how this may be applied for lessons about the human body.
Flynn, R. M., & Carr, G. A. (1994). Exploring classroom literature through drama: A specialist and a teacher collaborate. *Language Arts, 71*(1), 38–43.
  Describes drama learning strategies applicable to many curriculum areas and pieces of literature. Provides an in-depth look at a 45-minute session with second graders.
Friedlander, A. (1997). Young students investigate number cubes. *Teaching Children Mathematics, 4*(1), 6–11.
  Shares ways that math instruction can be made interesting and thematic.
Gagné, R., & Briggs, L. (1992). *Principles of instructional design*. New York: Holt, Rinehart & Winston.
  A thorough and authoritative text on the design of instruction. Although less useful for writing lesson plans, the authors describe nine events of instruction, not the seven presented in this chapter.
Karchmer, R. A., & Leu, D. D. (1999). The Miss Rumphius effect: Envisionments for literacy and learning that transform the Internet.
  In D. J. Leu, Jr. (Ed.), Exploring literacy on the Internet. *The Reading Teacher, 52*(6), 636–42.
  The following five web-based sources provide creative and effective ways to use the Internet to enhance your unit and lesson plans and your students' motivation to learn: Karchmer (1999); Rekrut (1999); Risinger (1999); Ritter (1999); Shiroma (2000); and Sprague (2000).
[2]Martin-Kniep, G. O., Feige, D. M., & Soodak, L. C. (1995). Curriculum integration: An expanded view of an abused idea. *Journal of Curriculum and Supervision, 10*(3), 227–49.
  Discusses various ways integration can be achieved and emphasizes that curriculum integration also causes some unintentional sacrifice of content, skills, or other aspects.

[1]Pardo, L. S., & Raphael, T. E. (1991). Classroom organization for instruction in content areas. *The Reading Teacher, 44*(8), 556–65.
  Notes that use of a variety of grouping strategies in a classroom is not sufficient to create independent and successful learners. Comprehension strategies and other activities must be carefully modeled and utilized in many instructional settings.

Pasch, M., Sparks-Langer, G., Gardner, T. G., Starko, A. J., & Moody, C. D. (1991). *Teaching as decision making: Instructional practices for the successful teacher.* New York: Longman.
  This text provides plenty of examples of unit and lesson plans for the beginning teacher—along with many practical tips on how to design a lesson.

Rekrut, M. D. (1999). Using the Internet in classroom instruction: A primer for teachers. *Journal of Adolescent & Adult Literacy, 42*(7), 546–57.

Ricklin, L. P., & Perfect-Miller, S. (1993, February). A dig that's good enough to eat. *Teaching: K–8,* 50–2.
  Describes an integrated lesson plan involving an "archeocake" loaded with "artifacts" from which to teach students about archaeological processes. Creative example of integrating several traditional disciplines and enhancing the inquiry process.

Risinger, C. F. (1999). Teaching social studies with the Internet. (ERIC Document Reproduction Service No. ED 435 582)

Ritter, N. (1999). Teaching interdisciplinary thematic units in language arts. *ERIC Digest D142.* Bloomington, IN: ERIC Clearinghouse on Reading, English, and Communication. (ERIC Document Reproduction Service No. ED 436 003)
  Recent trends toward thematic teaching can help teachers avoid pitfalls, but only if the themes which organize the unit are chosen carefully, and in ways that help students understand content connections and relationships to their own lives.

Roberts, P., & Kellough, R. (2004). *A guide for developing interdisciplinary thematic units* (3rd ed.). Upper Saddle River, NJ: Merrill/Prentice Hall.
  This book provides an up-to-date reference for writing ITUs that offers step-by-step directions and plenty of examples to guide the way.

Rule, A. C., & Sunal, C. S. (1994). *Buttoning up a hands-on history lesson, 7*(2), 8–11.
  Suggests that introducing young students (elementary) to history concepts is difficult because they have little reference for comprehending change over time. Discusses the uses of buttons for an inquiry-based activity designed to enhance student interest and learning.

Sardo-Brown, D. (1988). Teachers' planning. *The Elementary School Journal, 89,* 68–87.
  A report on how a sample of elementary school teachers actually used objectives in planning their lessons and units.

Scarnati, J. T. (1994). Interview with a wild animal: Integrating science and language arts. *Middle School Journal, 25*(4), 3–6.
  Describes an upper grade unit of study that involves writing and student imagination.

Shiroma, D. (2000). Using primary sources on the Internet to teach and learn history. (ERIC Document Reproduction Service No. ED 442 739)

Smith, J. L., & Johnson, H. (1994). Models for implementing literature in content studies. *The Reading Teacher, 48*(3), 198–209. Presents a framework for understanding and developing various types of literature-based units.

Sprague, C. (2000). An introduction to Internet resources for K–12 educators. Part 1: Information resources update 2000. (ERIC Document Reproduction Service No. ED 444 502)

Tomlinson, C. A. (2000). Differentiation of instruction in the elementary grades. *ERIC Digest.* Washington, DC: Office of Educational Research and Improvement & U.S. Department of Education. (ERIC Document Reproduction Service No. ED 443 572)
  Tomlinson presents a practical way in which lessons can be individualized or differentiated for groups of learners across four elements: content (what the student needs to learn or how the student will access information); process (activities in which the student will engage to master the content); products (projects that ask the student to rehearse, apply, and extend unit knowledge); and learning environment (the way the classroom works and feels).

Webre, E. C. (1995). Learning about science through poetry. *Teaching K–8.* 50–1.
  Summarizes numerous children's literature selections helpful for teaching science through poetry.

ACTIVE LEARNING

ENHANCE your teaching plan in any of the following time-honored ways—or use the list below to help you brainstorm other interesting activities for students to learn/share something new.

Chain Story: Each student takes a turn telling a portion of the content and stops whenever s/he desires. The next speaker picks up where the previous student left off.

Charades: Words allowed.

Choral Speaking: Groups or individuals speak together or in a specific sequence. Several options include:

1. *Refrain:* Leader speaks most of the lines and group repeats a refrain.
2. *Line-a-child* or *Line-a-group:* Each child or group speaks a couplet before the next group takes its turn.
3. *Antiphonal:* Two or more groups of speakers alternate in speaking a piece. Groups may be male and female, high and low pitches, etc. as needed for effect.
4. *Unison:* No subgrouping is used.
5. *Audience Cue:* Cue cards are used to involve the audience as in old-fashioned melodrama or in speaking specific refrains, etc.

Improvisation: No written script.

News Stories: Reporters report on informational events and key participants. The audiences can ask questions, and "experts" may bluff until someone catches them. They can also be restricted to giving only factual and correct answers.

Panel Discussions or Debates: Can be held between important participants of the same time era or differing eras. Can be focused on events and factual information or on the character's motivation, emotions, etc.

Pantomine: No words, no props (or few props).

Plot Completion: Students brainstorm what led to the story's beginning and what happened where the story leaves off.

Puppetry: Stick, whole body, drawings, paper bag, paper plate, finger, shadow, glove, sock, sewn, mix and match, marionettes, Styrofoam cups, etc.

Readers' Theater: Group members read from a script and interact with the audience but not one another.

Storytelling: Students tell stories in the grand old tradition, emphasizing voice, body, and emotion.

Talk Shows: Students pose as famous persons, inventors, experts in a particular field, etc., and are interviewed on "television" before a live "studio" audience.

Tape Recording/Radio Shows: Students record their presentations and can add sound effects, musical backgrounds, etc.

Videotaping: "Movies," "Commercials," "Film Previews," "Television Shows."

Gagné Lesson Plan Form

1. **Gain Attention:**
    Consider 1) "Opener" questions that amuse, bewilder, present an apparent contradiction or inconsistency; and 2) Diagrams, pictures, illustrations, scale models, and films to pique interest.

2. **Inform the Learner(s) of the Objective:**
    What is the behavioral outcome the students are to attain by the end of the lesson? How will it be measured/exhibited?

3. **Stimulate Recall of Prerequisite Learning:**
    Identify and activate key concepts underlying today's lesson.

4. **Present the Stimulus Material:**
    A) Authenticity
    B) Selectivity
    C) Variety (visual, oral, tactile; large group, small group, individual)

5. Elicit the Desired Behavior:
A) Nonevaluative atmosphere (perhaps every-student-response)
B) Brief
C) Written, oral, subvocal

6. Provide Feedback:
How will the learner feel affirmed? How will incorrect responses be revised?

7. Assess the Behavior:
Consider a test, quiz, homework, workbook, performance, lab, oral presentation, extended essay, research paper, independent practice, portfolio entry, etc.
A) Immediately, at the end of the lesson
B) At the end of the week
C) At the end of the unit

BRIDGES

Chapter 5
Direct Instruction Strategies

Chapter 5	A. *Personal, Dialogue, or Buddy Journals*	B. *Self-Directed Study Activities*	C. *Cooperative & Collaborative Ideas*	D. *Whole Class*
Introducing the Content	1. What makes a teacher/class interesting? 2. What makes you want to respond in class? What makes you choose to be silent? Does your participation pattern vary among classes? Why?	1. **WATCH** someone do a "direct instruction" lesson. What strengths or weaknesses do you note in the approach?	1. **BRAINSTORM** meanings for the terms "homework" and "busywork." How are the two similar? How are they different? What are the goals of each? **CREATE A CHART** (pp. 7–8) that compares/contrasts your ideas. You may want to differentiate between "ideal" and "less than ideal" uses of each.	1. Use a **COVERT RESPONSE TECHNIQUE** (p. 17) in today's lecture, perhaps with all or part of the chapter practice questions. **DISCUSS** how it feels to be able to respond "safely" as opposed to being "put on the spot" in class.

Chapter 5 continued	A. Personal, Dialogue, or Buddy Journals	B. Self-Directed Study Activities	C. Cooperative & Collaborative Ideas	D. Whole Class
Assimilating/ Reviewing the Content	3. What comes to mind when you hear the word "busywork"? How about the word "homework"? How are the two similar? How are they different? What are the goals of each? 4. How do you feel about grading work at the beginning of class? How many of your teachers did that?	2. **THINK** about the idea that "teaching is not telling." How do you reconcile that idea with the concept of direct instruction?	2. **LIST** the 7 steps of lesson planning according to Gagné. **CREATE A GRAPHIC** to show the direct instruction options for addressing each and **SHARE** with the class. 3. **ROLE PLAY** types of student responses and **CHART** ways to deal with them.	2. Return to the **BEHAVIORAL OBJECTIVE PLANNING SHEET** (p. 25) and **DRAW** in a line to divide each **OVAL** into Type 1 and Type 2 behaviors. **EXPLAIN** that Chapter 5 focuses on supporting Type 1 behaviors, and Chapter 6 focuses on Type 2 behaviors. As a class, **NOTE** the meaning of Type 1 and Type 2 behaviors somewhere on the planning sheet.

Chapter 5: Checking Your Understanding

True or False:

1. _____ Independent practice should help students internalize a behavior or response so that it becomes automatic.
2. _____ It is important to give detailed feedback to students as they begin to practice a new skill or behavior so they can avoid any errors.
3. _____ Direct instruction is most efficient for teaching Type 1 learning outcomes such as facts, rules, and action sequences.
4. _____ A good way to determine when to reteach a concept to the whole class is to see how many high and low performers made errors on the practice assignment.
5. _____ A teacher should determine what type of feedback to offer a student based on the correctness and surety of the student's response.
6. _____ Information taught in a direct instruction format is most easily tested through multiple choice, listing, matching, and fill-in exercises.
7. _____ Teachers should use the most powerful prompt possible to help learners perform, even if a less intrusive prompt may work.
8. _____ Programmed instruction, computer-assisted instruction, peer and cross-age tutoring, and some audiolingual approaches can also be used for direct instruction.

9. _____ A lecture-recitation format involves only teacher lectures and students' responses to questions.
10. _____ Direct instruction methods correlate highest with student achievement on standardized measures.
11. _____ Research has shown that most teachers begin direct instruction lessons with review and checking to find out if students have mastered task-relevant knowledge from the previous lesson.

Multiple Choice:

12. _____ Which of the following are the most common strategies for dealing with incorrect student responses? (Mark all that apply.)
   a. Ask students to repeat the correct response after you model it.
   b. Review key facts or rules required to achieve the solution.
   c. Ask students to recite by memory the steps required to solve a problem.
   d. Offer prompts or hints representing a partially correct answer.
   e. Use another problem and guide the student to the correct answer.

| 1. T | 2. F | 3. F | 4. T | 5. T | 6. T |
| 7. F | 8. T | 9. F | 10. T | 11. F | 12. b, d, e |

Chapter 5: Performance Assessment Ideas		
Individual	*Small Group*	*Whole Class*
1. **OBTAIN** a curriculum guide for an area in which you'd like to teach. **CHOOSE** a subject area and **PLAN A LESSON** you believe would best be accomplished through direct instruction. Include your lesson plan and your reflections on the process in your portfolio. 2. **OBSERVE** a lesson using the direct instruction method. **CRITIQUE** it from your understanding of direct instruction. Place your observation notes and critique in your portfolio.	1. **CHOOSE** several articles from those referenced in this chapter. Have each group member **READ** a different article (see **SUGGESTED READINGS,** p. 39) and **PREPARE A BRIEF SUMMARY** of how its content applies to the idea of direct instruction as you understand it. Have each group member **WRITE A 1–2 SENTENCE CRITIQUE** of the article's importance and the group member's delivery. Include a copy of the article, the summary, and the group critiques in your portfolio.	1. **CHOOSE** a lesson from this course (or another lesson all class members can experience, such as one on a videotape) and **EVALUATE** it for Type 1 and Type 2 behaviors. What do you notice about the lesson and the behaviors required? What would you change?

CHILDREN'S LITERATURE CONNECTION

Brown, M. W. (1949/1990). *The important book.* New York: HarperCollins.
>   *The predictable format of this book, "The important thing about _____ is that _____" lends itself to a number of reading/writing/sharing activities wherein students assign perspective and value to ideas.*

Cole, J. (1995). *Magic School Bus inside Ralphie.* New York: Scholastic.
>   *This and other* Magic School Bus *books suggest that direct instruction need not be "dry." Some others in the series include* Inside the Earth *(1987),* Inside the Human Body *(1989),* Ups and Downs *(1997),* Going Batty *(1996),* Inside a Beehive *(1996),* The Electric Field Trip *(1997),* Inside a Hurricane *(1995),* In the Time of the Dinosaurs *(1994),* Lost in the Solar System *(1990),* On the Ocean Floor *(1992), and* At the Waterworks *(1986).*

Pfister, M. (1998). *How Leo learned to be king.* New York: Scholastic.
>   *The animals tell Leo flat-out that he's not a good king. Sometimes the direct approach is the best for a change, as Leo and his friends discover.*

Willis, J. (1988). *Earthlets as explained by Professor Xargle,* New York: Dutton.
>   *Professor Xargle uses direct instruction and is anything but boring. He combines direct instruction with a field trip, once he has built important background. (This book can also be used to review Chapter 2 content and emphasize the importance of perspective. Questions such as "How do we look to Xargle's people?" "How do we look as teachers?" "How do our units look to students?" can help us "step back" and look at our planning from varied perspectives.)*

SUGGESTED READINGS

Bennett, D. (1982). Should teachers be expected to learn and use direct instruction? *Association for Supervision and Curriculum Development Update,* 24(4), 5.

A statement on some of the uses of direct instruction and when it is most likely to be effective.

Berghoff, B., & Egawa, K. (1991). No more "rocks": Grouping to give students control of their learning. *The Reading Teacher, 44*(8), 536–41.

Discusses pros and cons of traditional grouping methods and includes a helpful chart for expanding group assignment to include independent, paired, small group, and whole group instruction.

Berliner, D. (1982). Should teachers be expected to learn and use direct instruction? *Association for Supervision and Curriculum Development Update,* 24(4), 5.

A critical statement on when and where direct instruction is most applicable.

Brophy, J. (1982). Successful teaching strategies for the inner-city child. *Phi Delta Kappan, 63,* 527–30.

A case for direct instruction employing research results confirming its positive effects on the achievement of inner-city students.

Chambers, D. L. (1995). Improving instruction by listening to children. *Teaching Children Mathematics, 1*(6), 378–80.

Suggests that teachers need to attend more to students' responses and thinking. Gives examples of classroom dialogue where teachers listen well.

Dixon, M. E., & Rossie, J. C. (1995). A reading strategy for students with learning disabilities. *Teaching Exceptional Children, 27*(2), 10–4.

The authors describe how to model and teach a three-phase reading strategy for students with learning disabilities which involves students in asking questions about a story, discussing criteria for types of questions (fact, inference, opinion), and labeling the questions. Helps the reader see how a teacher can use direct instruction and modeling to help students assume the role of discussion leader in their own groups.

Gagné, R. M. (1985). *Conditions of learning and theory of instruction* (4th ed.). New York: Holt.

This classic text sets out many of the learning principles from which the direct instruction model was derived.

Gagné, R. M. (1992). *Principles of instructional design.* Orlando, FL: Harcourt Brace Jovanovich.

An excellent reference for preparing unit and lesson plans that include the direct instruction model.

Good, T., Grouws, D., & Ebmeier, H. (1983). *Active mathematics teaching.* New York: Longman.

An explanation of how best to apply direct instruction in mathematics.

Hadaway, N. L., & Young, T. A. (1994). Content literacy and language learning: Instructional decisions. *The Reading Teacher, 47*(7), 522–7.

Describes ways teachers can model the use of comprehension strategies for their students. Includes a number of teaching ideas and activities.

Jitendra, A. K., & Torgerson-Tubiello, R. (1997). Let's learn contractions! *Teaching Exceptional Children, 29*(4), 16–9.

The authors share how they used direct instruction to teach contractions to six low-performing second graders. They include details for planning similar lessons, along with a sample lesson plan.

Keegan, S., & Shrake, K. (1991). Literature study groups: An alternative to ability grouping. *The Reading Teacher, 44*(8), 542–7.

Describes how to implement, conduct, and evaluate literature study groups as an alternative to traditional ability grouping. The idea can be extended beyond reading of novels to reading of various texts in other disciplines.

Lindsley, O. R. (1992). Precision teaching: Discoveries and effects. *Journal of Applied Behavior Analysis, 24*(1), pp. 51–7.

The author describes a technique called "precision teaching," which contains many of the ingredients of the direct instruction model that have been found effective for teaching basic skills.

McKeachie, W. J. (1990). Learning, thinking, and Thorndike. *Educational Psychologist, 25,* 127–42.

Some of the most basic principles of learning and thinking are discussed from a direct instruction model.

Moss, B. (1995). Using children's nonfiction tradebooks as read-alouds. *Language Arts, 72*(2), 122–6.

Offers reasons for reading nonfiction aloud and provides steps for planning nonfiction read-aloud experiences.

Naughton, V. M. (1993/1994). Creative mapping for content reading. *Journal of Reading, 37*(4), 324–6.

Describes creative mapping as a pictorial version of semantic mapping as a tool to help students better understand content materials. Includes a description of how to model the process and a sample map.

Nelson, J. R., & Johnson, A. (1996). Effects of direct instruction, cooperative learning, and independent learning practices on the behavior of students with behavioral disorders: A comparative analysis. *Journal of Emotional & Behavioral Disorders, 4*(1), 53–62.

This somewhat technical research reports that direct instruction was more effective for behaviorally disordered students than was cooperative learning or independent learning. Students may enjoy reading through the study; imagining its application in classrooms they've seen, and drawing tentative conclusions about when to use direct instruction methods in their lesson planning.

Olson, M. W., & Gee, T. C. (1991). Content reading instruction in the primary grades: Perceptions and strategies. *The Reading Teacher, 45*(4), 298–307.

Discusses the importance of helping young children develop skill in reading information texts. Describes six strategies for helping students develop greater content reading proficiency.

Rosenshine, B. (1983). Teaching functions in instructional programs. *The Elementary School Journal, 83,* 335–51.

An oft-cited article that describes all of the functions of the direction instruction model as described in this chapter.

Spiegel, D. L. (1992). Blending whole language and systematic direct instruction. *The Reading Teacher, 46*(1), 38–44.

Summarizes what she believes to be the contributions of the whole language movement as well as the advantages of systematic direct instruction. Suggests that while many view the two as mutually exclusive or conflicting, bridges can and should be built by educators to take advantage of the strengths in both instructional approaches.

Werts, M. G., Wolery, M., Gast, D. L., & Holcombe, A. (1996). Sneak in some extra learning by using instructive feedback. *Exceptional Children, 28*(3), 70–1.

This brief and readable article explains how to use instructive feedback (presenting extra information during feedback following students' responses to direct instruction) to intentionally and methodically boost students' learning. The process involves identifying information to be supplied, deciding how to present the information, using the method consistently, and monitoring effects.

BRIDGES

Chapter 6
Indirect Instruction Strategies

Chapter 6	A. *Personal, Dialogue, or Buddy Journals*	B. *Self-Directed Study Activities*	C. *Cooperative & Collaborative Ideas*	D. *Whole Class*
Introducing the Content	1. What memories do you have of the "scientific method"? Are they positive? Why or why not? When did you use it? 2. Do you remember any "real discussions" in a class? What made them work? What makes some discussions fail?	1. **COMPARE/ CONTRAST** the idea of direct versus indirect instruction. What do you see as the advantages/drawbacks of each? With which are you more familiar? 2. **CONSIDER** what the term "constructivism" means to you. In what area(s) of your life have you constructed some of your own knowledge?	1. If you have met in the same group throughout this course, **MEET** with that group to **DISCUSS** how it has functioned. **COMPARE** your learning and experiences in the group activities with whole class and individual activities. What do you find? Do others in your group agree with you?" 2. **COMPARE** the **DIRECT INSTRUC-TION LESSON PLAN** (pp. 47–48) with the **GAGNÉ LESSON PLAN FORM** (pp. 33–34).	1. **CREATE** and **DISPLAY** an overhead transparency of workers doing construction. **DRAW A PARALLEL** with constructivist thought wherein learners construct personal meaning from interactions with their environments. **BRAINSTORM** the implications of a learner's environment in such a view (i.e., early experiences and the nature of social interactions will be pivotal, etc.).

*If you haven't met with the same people, meet in a group to discuss your group experiences in more general terms or to discuss how group work may have altered your experience.

Chapter 6 continued	A. Personal, Dialogue, or Buddy Journals	B. Self-Directed Study Activities	C. Cooperative & Collaborative Ideas	D. Whole Class
Assimilating/ Reviewing the Content	3. What does discovery learning mean to you? How does it COMPARE to the idea of inquiry learning or problem-solving curricula? 4. Have you ever experienced a student-centered approach to teaching which resulted in "pooled ignorance" (where the teacher failed to guide the instruction sufficiently)? HOW DID YOU FEEL about the experience? What role might curriculum guidelines play in helping teachers avoid such events?	3. **MAKE A VISUAL** which captures the content of Chapters 5 and 6 for you to use as a future teacher. 4. How would you **DEFINE** "social framing"? What **IMPLICATIONS** do you see for this concept in the setting where you hope to teach? 5. **READ** one or more articles on discussion referenced on pages 44–46. **WRITE** and **SHARE A RESPONSE** to the information.	3. **CREATE A VISUAL** for the roles of a teacher in indirect and direct settings. [1,2] **SHARE** your visual with the class. 4. With a partner, **THINK** of an example of direct/indirect instruction used in this course (or in another). Was it a good choice for the topic and the objective? Why or why not? 5. **ROLE PLAY** questioning using the search and discovery process. Use the **TALKING CHIPS** (p. 46) activity to encourage each group member to fully participate in the discussion.	2. **INTRODUCE** the idea of **PARAPHRASE PASSPORT** (p. 46) before the class discussion today. At the conclusion of the lesson, **REFLECT** on the success of the strategy in enhancing discussion.

Chapter 6: Checking Your Understanding

Multiple Choice:

1. _____ According to constructivist theories, indirect instruction is important because knowledge results:
   a. by forming rules and hypotheses about "reality" from one's own perspective
   b. from being exposed to the facts about the world as interpreted by others
   c. from careful, systematic memorization on one's personal timetable
   d. from students "telling" other students about the world

2. _____ Deductive reasoning skills are helpful for students because: (Mark all that apply)
   a. much information can be obtained by beginning with a theory and testing or experimenting with it to see how accurately it predicts events
   b. generalizations can be misleading if they are not carefully tested
   c. knowing that something generally occurs can alert us to watch for similar situations and act accordingly
   d. what occurs in one place is bound to occur in another

3. _____ Which of the following strategies are included in indirect instruction?
   a. cooperative learning and programmed instruction
   b. self-directed inquiry and cooperative learning
   c. inquiry learning and memorization
   d. discovery learning and step-by-step procedures

4. _____ A helpful way to think about and plan for constructivist approaches to learning is to present curriculum in:
   a. a step-by-step, logical sequence
   b. a prestructured unit of study
   c. a problem-solving format
   d. an open discussion or demonstration format

True or False:

5. _____ Deductive reasoning generally leads to greater levels of complexity because patterns and generalizations are accepted as fact.

6. _____ Students can be aided in taking responsibility for their own learning through opportunities to engage in self-evaluation.

7. _____ Indirect instruction is more complex than direct instruction with regard to teacher behavior, but not student behavior.

8. _____ A single, good question is the centerpiece of indirect instruction.

9. _____ Student dialogue plays an important part in the process of indirect instruction.

10. _____ Teachers should avoid sharing their personal feelings and experiences related to a specific lesson.

11. _____ Indirect instruction is correlated with positive student attitudes.

1. a   2. a,b,c   3. b   4. c   5. F   6. T   7. F   8. F   9. T   10. F   11. T

Chapter 6: Performance Assessment Ideas		
Individual	*Small Group*	*Whole Class*
1. **REFLECT** on your own experiences with cooperative/collaborative learning either in this course or in another setting. How did the experiences **COMPARE** to the information in this chapter? What questions do you have about the processes? What plans do you have for using such strategies in your own teaching? Why do you feel this way?	1. **BRAINSTORM** two or three teaching situations for which a cooperative/collaborative approach would be appropriate. **WRITE** a short vignette for each, along with how you envision the strategy working. **PRESENT** your ideas to the class and revise where needed. **TEST** your ideas if there is an available setting.	1. **PERUSE** cooperative learning manuals and books and select 2–3 team-building activities for the class. **PARTICIPATE** in the activities and **DEBRIEF** regarding their effectiveness in helping you feel a part of the group. **BRAINSTORM** other ideas about what helps you feel included in a group and **COMPILE** a class list.

CHILDREN'S LITERATURE CONNECTION

Gilman, P. (1992). *Something from nothing*. New York: Scholastic.
   Joseph watches his grandfather as he creates new items from his baby blanket—until the blanket is reduced to the size of a button. He learns to create stories in the same way—suggesting the role of indirect instruction in student learning.
Slepian, J., & Seidler, A. (1967). *The hungry thing*. New York: Scholastic.
   Just as the young boy aids the town by figuring out the pattern in the Thing's communication, so our students are engaged in and aided in their learning by being allowed to "discover" and "figure out" patterns in the content we study and share together. [There is also a second book by the same authors, The Hungry Thing Returns. *(1990). New York: Scholastic.*

SUGGESTED READINGS

Aker, D. (1992). From runned to ran: One journey toward a critical literacy. *Journal of Reading, 36*(2), 104–12.
   Describes his evolving understanding as he gained a more constructivist view of reading. Can be helpful in helping to clarify differences between traditional views of reading comprehension and constructivist views of students creating their own meanings.
Barton, J. (1995). Conducting effective classroom discussion. *Journal of Reading, 38*(5), 346–50.
   Discusses the complexity of leading successful discussions and offers specific strategies for enhancing class discussions.

Bertheau, M. (1994). The most important thing is . . . . *Teaching Children Mathematics (92)* 112–5.

Describes how a teacher follows the children's lead to integrate literature and curriculum in discovery learning about shapes. A useful example of how teachers can build on student interests to develop integrated curriculum lessons. (Refers to The Important Book, *see Children's Literature Connection Chapter 5, p. 38).*

Brooks, J. (1990). Teachers and students: Constructivists forging connections. *Educational Leadership, 47*(5), 68–71.

This article explains how constructivist teaching and learning can be used to promote integrated bodies of knowledge.

Burnette, J. (1999). Critical behaviors and strategies for teaching culturally diverse students. *ERIC/OSEP Digest E 584.* Arlington, VA: ERIC Clearinghouse on Disabilities and Gifted Education. (ERIC Document Reproduction Service No. ED 435 147)

Among other important recommendations, Burnette recommends concluding lessons or units with the same advance organizer that introduced them to help diverse students better envision where instruction began and ended.

Churchwell, G., Weller, C. J., & Sommer, P. (1997). Hometown discovery: Learning locally, thinking globally. *T.H.E. Journal, 25*(1), 43–6.

Describes a project in New York that engages secondary students in discovery learning, the products of which are then shared with fourth-grade students studying local history.

Curran-Everett, D. (1997). The Möbius band: An unusual vehicle for science exploration. *Science and Children, 34*(5), 22–5.

Describes ways to explore the Möbius band with children in a discovery format.

Dillon, J. (1987). *Questioning and discussion: A multidisciplinary study.* Norwood, NJ: Ablex.

Presentation of the research and logic that underlies the discussion method.

[2]Eeds, M., & Peterson, R. (1991). Teacher as curator: Learning to talk about literature. *The Reading Teacher, 45*(2), 118–26.

Suggests that teachers think of reading as a transaction between a reader and a text, and consider their own role in the reading process from new vantage points. Includes excerpts from student discussions and illustrates ways to interact with students.

Giaconia, R. (1987). Open versus formal methods. In M. J. Dunkin (Ed.), *International encyclopedia of teaching and teacher education.* New York: Pergamon.

An introduction to some of the most important differences between the direct and indirect models.

Harris, K. R., & Graham, S. (1996). Memo to constructivists: Skills count, too. *Educational Leadership, 53*(5), 26–30.

The authors of this article critique their daughter's experience in a whole language school and make suggestions for integrating various educational philosophies. Students may enjoy reading this article and role playing various perspectives (e.g., whole language teacher, skills-only teacher, concerned parents).

Joyce, B., & Wells, M. (1992). *Models of teaching.* Upper Saddle River, NJ: Merrill/Prentice Hall.

A review of many of our most popular styles of teaching—a good complement to the two models described in this chapter.

Kamii, C., & Lewis, B. (1993, January). The harmful effects of algorithms . . . in primary arithmetic. *Teaching: K–8*, 36–8.

Helps elucidate a constructivist view of learning by explaining how children must create a personal understanding of math concepts rather than memorize one.

Knodt, J. S. (1997). A think tank cultivates kids. *Educational Leadership, 55*(1), 35–7.

Basing their work on Gardner's multiple-intelligence theory, a Virginia school provides a hands-on discovery room for children to explore various abilities. Describes the philosophy behind the room and several activities within it.

Michaels, S., & Collins, J. (1984). Oral discourse styles: Classroom interaction and the acquisition of literacy. In D. Tannen (Ed.), *Coherence in spoken and written discourse.* Norwood, NJ: Ablex.

An introduction to the many styles of discourse that can be used during indirect instruction.

[1]O'Flahavan, J. F. (1994/1995). Teacher role options in peer discussions about literature. *The Reading Teacher, 48*(4), 354–6.
  Suggests an outline for a 30-minute session including discussion about a particular text. Suggests that teachers adopt the role best fitting the needs of a particular group, choosing from coaching, scaffolding, or combining both.

Ross, M. E. (1997). Scientists at play. *Science and Children, 34*(8), 35–8.
  Offers strategies for facilitating the explorations of young children including support of open-ended inquiry, safe supervision, and celebrating wonder.

Saunders, W., O'Brien, G., Lennon, D., & McLean, J. (1999). *Successful transition into mainstream English: Effective strategies for studying literature.* Washington, DC: Center for Research on Education, Diversity and Excellence.
  These authors find that advance organizers are especially helpful for students from diverse cultures and English Language Learners when the organizer includes links between familiar concepts and the new content to be learned.

Schweinhart, L. J. (1997). Child-initiated learning activities for young children living in poverty. *ERIC Digest*, EDO-PS-97-23.
  Notes the value of indirect and child-centered instruction over time, especially with young at-risk children. Suggests the need for basing early educational activities on constructivist principles.

Slavin, R. (1987). Small group methods. In M. J. Dunkin (Ed.), *International encyclopedia of teaching and teacher education.* New York: Pergamon.
  An overview of some ideas on how to use small groups to promote a cooperative classroom environment.

Swift, K. (1993). Try Reading Workshop in your classroom. *The Reading Teacher, 46*(5), 366–71.
  A sixth-grade teacher discusses her experiences in implementing a Reading Workshop in her classroom.

Tanne, D. (1986). *That's not what I meant!* New York: Morrow.
  Discusses the concept of "framing" and how it can determine the meaning of your message.

Watson, B., & Konicek, R. (1990). Teaching for conceptual change: Confronting children's experience. *Phi Delta Kappan, 71*, 680–5.
  An introduction to constructivist thought and logic with some interesting examples from the classroom.

ACTIVE LEARNING

TALKING CHIPS is a cooperative learning activity designed to encourage participation by each group member. It proceeds in the following manner:

1. Pose a question for which there is not a clear, literal answer.
2. Give each member in the group a stack of colored papers or chips (each member receives a different color).
3. Have groups discuss the question, each member placing a chip in the center pile whenever s/he speaks.
4. Have groups respond to the question as a class, summarizing their group's ideas.
5. Have students compare their chip piles. Ideal piles should include a fairly balanced grouping of chips.

Sources:
This material has been adapted from the following book with permission from Kagan Publishing & Professional Development: Kagan, Spencer. *Cooperative Learning.* San Clemente, CA: Resources for Teachers, 1994. Templeton, Shane, *Teaching the Integrated Language Arts.* Copyright (©) 1991 by Houghton Mifflin Company. Reprinted with permission.
1(800) 933-2667; www.KaganOnline.com/.
(Numbered Heads Together, Kagan, 1994)

PARAPHRASE PASSPORT is another cooperative learning activity to encourage better discussions. After someone has contributed an idea to the group discussion, another person must correctly restate that idea before contributing his or her own idea.

Direct Instruction Lesson Plan

1. **Daily Review and Checking Previous Day's Work:**

2. **Presenting and Structuring:**
   Part-to-whole, sequential, combinatorial, comparative; rule-example-rule

3. **Guided Student Practice:**
   Nonevaluative-covert; feedback prompt, wrong answer conversion plans

4. **Feedback and Correctives:**

5. **Independent Practice:**
   A) Let students know the reason for doing the practice
   B) Brief, nonevaluative, supportive
   C) Ensure success
   D) Receive feedback (how will students receive it?)
   E) Progress, challenge, variety planned for

6. **Weekly and Monthly Reviews:**

BRIDGES

KNOWLEDGE	Chapter 7 Questioning Strategies	ACTIVITY

Chapter 7	A. *Personal, Dialogue, or Buddy Journals*	B. *Self-Directed Study Activities*	C. *Cooperative & Collaborative Ideas*	D. *Whole Class*
Introducing the Content	1. Can a question be used as a punishment? As a reward? Have you ever **EXPERIENCED** either? What do you recall about the experience(s)?	1. Does asking questions really enhance learning? Why do you **FEEL** this way? 2. Try reading this chapter using the **SQ3R** technique (p. 54) and asking yourself questions. What did you notice about your experience?	1. **THINK BACK** to the **WRITTEN CONVERSATION** activity on the first day of class (pp. x–xi). What did you learn about the questions you asked after you heard others share their information? **DO** the activity again in small groups and **ASK "BETTER" QUESTIONS** this time. What implications do you see from this experience for improving your ability to pose helpful questions to your future students?	1. Introduce and do the **MODIFIED REQUEST** procedure (p. 54) for this chapter and an upcoming test in the course. 2. **COMPLETE** a "pop quiz" like **"HOW IT WORKS"** (p. 57). **DISCUSS** how most students answered each question correctly, in spite of limited comprehension of the piece. **LEAD** into a discussion of assessment issues, especially those of traditional assessment.

Chapter 7 continued	A. Personal, Dialogue, or Buddy Journals	B. Self-Directed Study Activities	C. Cooperative & Collaborative Ideas	D. Whole Class
Assimilating/ Reviewing the Content	2. In your experience, how long do teachers generally wait for students to respond to their questions? How long should they wait? Why? 3. **THINK BACK** to ways teachers determined who to call on in school. What patterns did you like? Dislike? Why?	3. **CONSIDER** the idea of cultural wait times for questions and answers. What feels comfortable to you in a conversational setting? In an academic setting? **SURVEY** several peers and see if you find any differences among them. 4. **READ** the information on **QARs** (pp. 55–56). How might you **APPLY** this information to your teaching goals? To your personal learning strategies?	2. **BRAINSTORM** all the reasons teachers ask questions. **CATEGORIZE** your responses and then **COMPARE** them to those in your text. Did you think of any your author didn't? 3. **DISCUSS** the following questions in pairs or small groups: Do convergent and divergent questions have right/wrong answers? Why or why not? 4. **IMPROVISE** a classroom scene and **ROLE PLAY** a teacher asking probes to help a student extend his or her thinking. **SHARE** your improvisation with the class and **DEBRIEF** on the way your "instructor" responded to the student.	3. **ASK** the class the following questions and **LIST** their responses on the chalkboard: What is a question? When is it effective? 4. **USE DIFFERENT LENGTHS OF WAIT TIME** throughout the lesson today. **DRAW ATTENTION** to these variations and **DEBRIEF.** 5. **BRAINSTORM** teacher behaviors that defeat the power of questioning. **LIST** responses on the chalkboard to lead into a discussion of the topic. 6. **DEBATE** the following topic: Teachers should require **all** students to participate in answering questions in class.

Chapter 7: Checking Your Understanding

Match the following terms with your own definitions or summary statements taken from the text:

Analysis question	Comprehension question	Evaluation question	Synthesis question
Type 1 behaviors	Application question	Probe	Type 2 behaviors
Knowledge question	Participation structure	Divergent question	Convergent question
	Wait time		

True or False:

1. _____ According to Rowe, there are two kinds of wait time—the time a learner is given to respond to a question, and the time after a learner's response until the teacher speaks.
2. _____ Questions should encourage students to think about and act upon the material you have structured and presented.
3. _____ Divergent questions have more than one response, because all responses to them are correct.
4. _____ 60–70% of all school time is devoted to questions and answers.
5. _____ Teachers often reward an answer to a question when it is one they expect.
6. _____ One reason higher level questioning in classrooms may not appear to influence student achievement is that student achievement is often measured using standardized tests which often test for lower level, recall knowledge.
7. _____ Teachers should respond to questions and answers quickly to keep the flow of the class moving.
8. _____ Most questions teachers ask of students require only simple recall of facts.
9. _____ Comfortable or appropriate wait time may differ across cultures.

1. T   2. T   3. F   4. F   5. T   6. T   7. F   8. T   9. T

Chapter 7: Performance Assessment Ideas		
Individual	*Small Group*	*Whole Class*
1. **WRITE** a brief, reflective piece on what you have learned about preparing for tests. What do you look for in order to predict what will be on a teacher's first test? How do you prepare for subsequent tests? How do you prepare for different kinds of test questions? Do you prefer to study alone or in groups? Why? How does your test experience inform you as a future teacher?	1. In your group, **BRAINSTORM** a set of questions for this chapter and **MAKE A TEST** for the class. **SCORE** the "tests" and then **CRITIQUE** the questions. You might use a code on the test to indicate the group source for the question to facilitate feedback and understanding afterward. What did you learn about your test-writing skills? What would you do differently next time?	1. **READ** the chapter and **WRITE** at least two questions you could ask in class. Come to class with the questions, and try to **ASK** at least one of them. At the end of the discussion/lecture, **COMPARE** the questions each person brought. What do you notice about the questions? Was it helpful to come to class with specific questions in mind? Why or why not?

CHILDREN'S LITERATURE CONNECTION

Geisel, T. (Dr. Seuss). (1961, 1989). *What was I scared of?* New York: Scholastic.
> *The author discovers through questions and experiences that the unknown can become familiar.*

Palatini, M. *Piggie pie!* New York: Clarion Books.
> *The witch's faulty questioning strategies fail to help her understand what's really happening.*

Parish, P. (1963). *Amelia Bedelia.* New York: Harper & Row.
> *Vocabulary is an essential part of communication and understanding, as Amelia and her employers discover.*

Steig, W. (1984). *CDC?* Toronto: HarperCollins Canada.
> *Share some of the pages of this book with students using overhead transparencies. As they figure out the meanings, ask them to share their level of involvement and satisfaction in answering the question of what each page meant.*

SUGGESTED READINGS

Baloche, L. (1994). Breaking down the walls. Integrating creative questioning and cooperative learning into the social studies. *The Social Studies, 85*(1), 25–30.
> *Offers suggestions on how to ask questions using specific strategies. Illustrates with actual classroom dialogue and examples.*

Brown, G., & Wragg, E. (1993). *Questioning.* London: Routledge.
> *An update of research and practice on questioning with many examples of questioning strategies for the classroom.*

Brualdi, A. C. (1998). Classroom questions. *ERIC Digest.* College Park, MD: ERIC Clearinghouse on Assessment and Evaluation. (ERIC Document Reproduction Service No. ED 422 407)

This author provides a good summary of all the different types of questions that you can pose to pique your student learning and match the goals of your lesson.

Dillon, J. T. (1988). *Questioning and teaching: A manual of practice.* New York: Teachers College Press.

A valuable text for the beginning teacher, with many exercises and problems for practicing the fine art of questioning.

Doneau, S. (1987) Soliciting. In M. J. Dunkin (Ed.), *International encyclopedia of teaching and teacher education.* New York: Pergamon.

An overview of the many ways teachers can solicit responses from their students during a lesson.

Ezell, H. K., Kohler, F. W., Jarzynka, M., & Stratin, P. S. (1992). Use of peer-assisted procedures to teach QAR reading comprehension strategies to third-grade children. *Education & Treatment of Children, 15*(3), 205–27.

Although a bit technical, this report describes a peer interaction approach to teaching third grade students to use QAR. Students may find some of the study ideas applicable in their settings and may enjoy brainstorming ways to use QAR in teaching.

Gilles, C., Dickinson, J., McBride, C., & Vandover, M. (1994). Discussing our questions and questioning our discussions: Growing into literature study. *Language Arts, 71*(7), 499–508.

Notes that getting "grand conversations" going in classrooms takes persistence, reflection, and adaptability. Shares stories of three teachers' efforts to encourage student discussion.

Gillespie, C. (1990). Questions about student-generated questions. *Journal of Reading, 34*(4), 250–7.

Discusses the value of helping students generate their own questions for reading and offers strategies for teaching them to do so.

Hunkins, F. P. (1989). *Teaching thinking through effective questioning.* Boston: Christopher-Gordon.

An excellent reference for learning how to raise questions at higher levels of cognitive complexity.

King, A. (1995). Designing the instructional process to enhance critical thinking across the curriculum. *Teaching of Psychology, 22*(1), 13–7.

Although the author describes the use of questioning strategies in a university setting, ideas can be adapted to other contexts.

Manzo, A. V., & Manzo, U. C. (1990). Note Cue: A comprehensive and participation training strategy. *Journal of Reading, 33*(8), 608–11.

Details a structured approach for helping students learn to ask and answer questions and comment in class in more successful ways. The authors suggest that the strategy is especially well-suited for ESL, at-risk, and culturally different students.

McIntosh, M. E., & Draper, R. J. (1995). Applying the Question-Answer Relationship strategy in mathematics. *Journal of Adolescent & Adult Literacy, 39*(2), 120–31.

McIntosh, M. E., & Draper, R. J. (1996). Using the Question-Answer Relationship strategy to improve students' reading of mathematics texts. *Clearing House, 69*(3), 154–62.

The authors provide examples of learning experiences that integrate the QAR strategy with mathematics content and offer directions on how to create a unit that integrates strategy instruction with content instruction.

Power, B. (1997). The answer to better writing? Better questions! *Instructor, 108*(4), 60–1.

Suggests that asking questions that encourage more thinking and writing will help children accomplish more as a result of writing conferences. Offers specific questions and examples.

Redfield, D., & Rousseau, E. (1981). A meta-analysis of experimental research of teacher questioning behavior. *Review of Educational Research, 51,* 237–45.

A comprehensive review of research summarizing the most consistent findings on teacher questioning behavior.

Sullivan, P., & Clarke, D. (1991). Catering to all abilities through "good" questions. *Arithmetic Teacher, 39*(2), 14–5.

Notes that "good" questions require students to do more than simply remember a strategy and discusses how questions can be used to address a range of student abilities.

Tobin, K. (1980). The effect of an extended teacher wait-time on science achievement. *Journal of Research in Science Teaching, 17,* 469–75.

An interesting report of research that shows the influence that wait time can have on your students' behavior.

Tower, C. (2000). Questions that matter: Preparing elementary students for the inquiry process. *The Reading Teacher, 53*(7), 550–7.

This author focuses on questions that can inspire young learners to think and inquire beyond the traditional curriculum you may be teaching.

Ward, C. (1997). Never give 'em a straight answer. *Science and Children, 35*(3), 46–9.

Describes ways the Socratic method can be used to encourage students to notice more about their environment.

Watts, M., Gould, G., & Alsop, S. (1997). Questions of understanding: Categorizing pupils' questions in science. *School Science Review, 79*(286), 57–63.

Submits that student questions provide important information which can help teachers better address student needs.

Wilen, W. (1991). *Questioning skills for teachers* (3rd ed.). Washington, DC: National Education Association.

A revised edition of a practical and classic text on questioning with many specific examples for the elementary and secondary classroom.

ACTIVE LEARNING

SQ3R is a mnemonic first suggested as an aid for college students in studying their texts. The process follows five steps:

1. **Survey:** Students look over the material to be read, thinking about headings, glance at figures and graphs, etc. to determine the main idea of the passage.
2. **Question:** Students turn each section heading into a question they seek to answer as they read.
3. **Read:** Students read the passage, seeking to answer their questions.
4. **Recite:** Students review periodically during their reading by reciting questions and answers in their heads. This helps them maintain focus and check for understanding.
5. **Review:** Students attempt to answer their questions without looking back at the text. They then refer to the text where needed.

MODIFIED REQUEST is a cooperative learning procedure designed to encourage students to ask their own questions and direct their own learning. The procedure is outlined below:

1. Tell students the topic of the day.
2. Give students 1–2 minutes to write questions about it.
3. Have students ask you questions about the topic.
4. Answer each question fully. Pose no questions yourself.
5. Invite students to ask more questions.

Source: This material has been adapted from the following book with permission from Kagan Publishing & Professional Development: Kagan, Spencer. *Cooperative Learning.* San Clemente, CA: Resources For Teachers, 1994. 1(800) 933-2667; www.KaganOnline.com/.

(Numbered Heads together, Kagan, 1994)

QARs (QUESTION-ANSWER-RELATIONSHIPS) is a helpful mnemonic for teaching students how to better comprehend what they read. Students learn that answers to questions come from different sources: the text and their own experiences. Raphael (1986) calls these "In the Book" and "In My Head." Within each category are two subcategories.

For the "In the Book" category, the answer may be: a) stated explicitly in the text, within a single sentence of text: or b) available from the text but require the reader to put together information from different sentences to determine it. The former is called "Right There." The latter can be called either "Think and Search" or "Putting It Together."

The "In My Head" category can also be divided into two types, once students have a clear understanding that their background knowledge is a relevant source of information for answering questions. The two categories are: a) "Author and You"; and b) "On My Own." The two figures on pages 55 and 56 help illustrate these relationships.

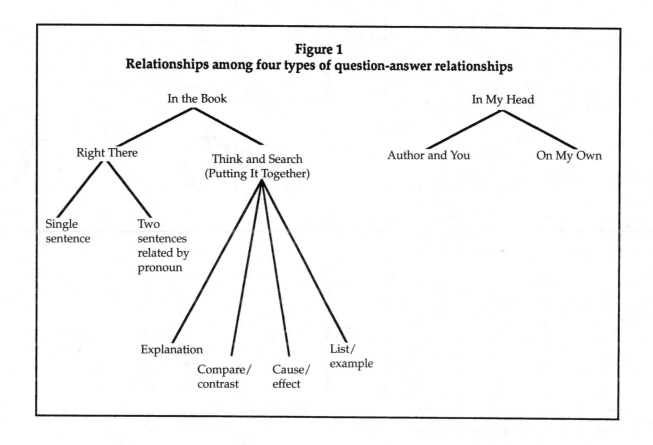

Figure 1
Relationships among four types of question-answer relationships

Figure 2
Illustrations to explain QARs to students

In the Book QARs

Right There
The answer is in the text, usually easy to find.
The words used to make up the question and
words used to answer the question are Right
There in the same sentence.

One day there was . . . So, Jack rode a horse to school today!	What did Jack ride to school today? (a horse)

Think and Search
(Putting It Together)
The answer is in the story, but you need to put
together different story parts to find it. Words for
the question and words for the answer are not
found in the same sentence. They come from
different parts of the text.

First, you get some bread. Second, you get a knife. Third, you get the peanut butter	How do you make a peanut butter sandwich?

In My Head QARs

Author and You
The answer is not in the story. You need to think
about what you already know, what the author
tells you in the text, and how it fits together.

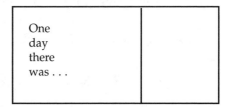

On My Own
The answer is not in the story. You can even
answer the question without reading the story.
You need to use your own experience.

Source: Raphael, Taffy, E. (1986, February). Teaching question answer relationships revisited. *The Reading Teacher, 39*(6), 516–22.

How It Works (Radio Passage)

The scope calibrator is basically a simple solid-state astable multivibrator designed to close tolerances. Transistors Q2 and Q3 comprise the multivibrator, whose frequency is determined essentially by the values of the timing components C1, C2, R3, and R4. The nominal 1020-Hz frequency can be reduced to an exact 1000-Hz signal by merely shunting C1 and C2 with a 20-pf. capacitor.

Emitter follower Q4 serves to isolate the multivibrator from the load effects of the output circuit while functioning as an impedence-matching device. Transistor Q1 serves only as a battery condition indicator. It is employed in an emitter follower configuration with a 10-volt lamp (I1) serving both as an indicator and as the emitter resistor.

As the source battery deteriorates, its output gradually approaches the zener (d1) voltage, reducing Q1's base bias and thus causing the lamp to glow more and more dimly. This can be observed by pressing the battery test switch (S2). However, because the calibrator would normally be used only on occasion rather than continuously, the life of the battery can be expected to approach its no-use shelf-life.

1. The scope calibrator is designed to
   a. receive radio messages
   b. close tolerances
   c. transmit radar signals

2. The frequency of the multivibrator is determined essentially by
   a. the values of the timing components
   b. the number of times the calibrator is used
   c. the condition of the battery indicator

3. The frequency of the multivibrator can be reduced to an exact 1000-Hz signal by
   a. redirecting the voltage of the emitter follower
   b. shunting C1 and C2 with a 20-pf. capacitor
   c. avoiding the deterioration of the battery

4. Transistor Q1 serves only as
   a. a reciprocal multivibrator
   b. a signal reflector
   c. a battery condition indicator

5. As the source battery deteriorates,
   a. the lamp glows more and more dimly
   b. the battery switch reverses its primary polarity
   c. the emitter follower is replaced by the emitter resistor

6. The life of the battery can be expected to approach shelf-life because
   a. the calibrator draws very little voltage
   b. the calibrator would normally be used occasionally
   c. the calibrator operates on low amperage

Source: Forman, Frederick, and Nawracaj, Edward. "Build: Solid-State Scope Calibrator." *Popular Electronics*, vol. 24 (June 1966), pp. 61–4.

BRIDGES

**Chapter 8
Self-Directed Learning**

Chapter 8	A. *Personal, Dialogue, or Buddy Journals*	B. *Self-Directed Study Activities*	C. *Cooperative & Collaborative Ideas*	D. *Whole Class*
Introducing the Content	1. Are you a self-starter? Does this ability/way of being vary in your life (e.g., you're a self-starter in art, but not in math, etc.)? 2. How do you feel when teachers open up study options in a particular course?	1. **SURVEY** your friends and/or neighbors regarding their study/learning strategies. What did you discover? Don't forget to **INCLUDE YOUR OWN APPROACHES** in your research. 2. What does the term "motivation" mean to you? How is motivation related to intrinsic and extrinsic rewards? Can you "motivate" another? **PERUSE** an article on motivation (see **Suggested Readings** for this chapter, p. 62)	1. Work with a partner to **COMPLETE THE STUDY GUIDE** (p. 68) for this chapter. **DEBRIEF** on whether the guide was useful to you as a learner.	1. **MODEL RECIPROCAL TEACHING** (pp. 65–66) with a passage. **DISCUSS** the gradual release of responsibility involved in this approach. **DEBRIEF** pros and cons of the approach.

Chapter 8 continued	A. Personal, Dialogue, or Buddy Journals	B. Self-Directed Study Activities	C. Cooperative & Collaborative Ideas	D. Whole Class
Assimilating/ Reviewing the Content	3. How do you "learn" best? Is that the same as how you "study" best? 4. How did you arrive at your current learning/studying strategies? Are there any which you feel need revision?	or one you find yourself. Does the information alter any of your views? How? 3. MAP key ideas (pp. 7–8) of the chapter or MAKE A SET OF NOTES you think would help you or your peers recall information in this chapter. REFLECT on the process you used: What did you do and how did it work?	2. Work with a partner or small group to CREATE A SIMPLE GRAPHIC, POEM, OR SONG SUMMARIZING KEY CONCEPTS in this chapter and present it to the class (p. 67). 3. SHARE a favorite/ useful study strategy with your group. Try to share it through a DIALOGUE which actually MODELS the strategy. What did you discover?	2. Ask students to EXPLAIN, from a constructivist view, how an independent learner is developed. DISCUSS the role of speech in learning at an interpersonal and intrapersonal level. 3. BRAINSTORM dialogue patterns that have occurred in class. Why is dialogue so important? STRESS the idea that it's hard to develop your own voice and make decisions if you don't trust in yourself, if you only learn to "parrot" the teacher, if you are not allowed to speak, etc.

Multiple Choice:

1. _____ To successfully demonstrate mental procedures, teachers should (mark all that apply):
   a. focus the learner's attention on the skill to be learned
   b. speak in educational terms when demonstrating so students hear and can use the proper academic terms
   c. combine steps of the process to simplify ideas
   d. work to make demonstrations particularly memorable in some way

2. _____ Inner speech does *not* help learners:
   a. guide their actions
   b. think about their thinking
   c. internalize ideas from their experiences
   d. maintain dependence upon teacher prompts

3. _____ A good way for teachers to enhance self-directed learning among culturally diverse students is:
   a. involve students in dialogues with one another and the teacher in addition to explaining and lecturing
   b. present important material in a clear, direct instruction format
   c. respond quickly to any student error with evaluative information to correct the problem
   d. group students according to similar backgrounds and lecture to their needs

4. _____ A learner's zone of maximum response opportunity is:
   a. a special learning environment in progressive schools
   b. a mental or physical activity that if simulated by a teacher brings a learner's response to the next level of refinement of which s/he is capable at the moment
   c. a kind of response indicating a student's best, unaided effort

True or False:

5. _____ The reason cognitive learning strategies are so important is because they provide specific ways for students to learn and remember specific content: They offer a carefully tailored approach for learning special subjects.

6. _____ In mental modeling a teacher demonstrates verbally the reasoning s/he used to solve a particular problem to help students apply similar reasoning in their own thinking.

7. _____ A good teaching strategy for helping students learn to think is to ask students to share how they arrived at a particular concept or solution to a problem.

8. _____ There are general approaches for solving problems (such as IDEAL), that can be taught to students to aid them in solving problems in a number of disciplines or subject areas.

9. _____ The term "metacognition" usually refers to a teacher's mental processes involved in planning a successful lesson.

10. _____ Teacher mediation means intervening between two students engaged in a personal conflict to help calm them.

11. _____ Functional failure can be a desirable event in a classroom.

     1. a, d   2. d   3. a   4. b   5. F   6. T   7. T   8. T   9. F   10. F   11. T

Chapter 8: Performance Assessment Ideas		
Individual	*Small Group*	*Whole Class*
1. **READ** all or part of Chapter 8 and **PAY CLOSE ATTENTION TO YOUR MENTAL PROCESSES.** What kinds of things do you notice yourself doing before you read? During? After? **WRITE** a short reflection on what you discovered. 2. **CHOOSE A TEXT** you will be studying (or teaching) and **CREATE A STUDY GUIDE** for one of the chapters or sections. What did you discover as you worked on the guide?	1. **CHOOSE A SHORT PASSAGE** from a professional journal, children's literature book*, newspaper, magazine, etc. **READ** it and determine where a less experienced reader might have difficulty understanding the message. **SHARE** the passage with a small group and **"TALK THROUGH"** how you make sense of the passage, especially those areas where you feel a student might have difficulty. What do you see as the value of "mental modeling" in this activity? How might this insight apply to you as a future teacher? 2. **READ** the article[1] referenced below. **DIFFERENTIATE** between teacher hearing and teacher listening. What implications does this piece have for helping students feel greater motivation and academic success? What differences do you see between listening to and listening for?	1. **LISTEN** as the course instructor models a particular learning strategy. **THINK** about what you are hearing and how this modeling helps or doesn't help you as a learner. What insights do you have? **WRITE** a short reflection about your thinking.

*Some children's literature books from which you may want to work are listed with an asterisk in the Suggested Readings section.

CHILDREN'S LITERATURE CONNECTION

Hoffman, M. (1991). *Amazing Grace*. New York: Penguin Books.
   With wise guidance, Grace capitalizes on her natural abilities. The same is true for students with whom we work—much of what we consider "motivation" involves coming to know students and offer opportunities for scholastic experiences to build upon their personal knowledge and interests.
Johnston, T. (1994). *Amber on the mountain*. New York: Dial Books for Young Readers.
   Amber is determined to learn to write, so she can communicate with her friend. Motivation springs from real values and needs.
Lionni, L. (1960). *Inch by inch*. New York: Scholastic.
   The inchworm has an idea that takes him out of harm's way—suggests the value of ideas and environments where they thrive.
Say, A. (1996). *Emma's rug*. Boston: Houghton Mifflin.
   Emma learns where the source of her art talent really is, just as we hope our students will discover their talents.
Shulevitz, U. (1978). *The treasure*. New York: Scholastic.
   An old man learns by experience that his "treasure" is right under his nose.
Walsh, E. S. (1989). *Mouse paint*. San Diego: Harcourt Brace Jovanovich.
   The mice discover all kinds of color combinations as they experiment. (Can also be used with Chapter 9 and cooperative learning.)
Williams, K. L. (1990). *Galimoto*. New York: Trumpet Club.
   Hondi is determined to collect enough wire to make a galimoto. Demonstrates the motivation of problem-solving when it derives from something a student truly cares about.

SUGGESTED READINGS

Anderson, L. H., & Midgley, C. (1998). Motivation and middle school students. *ERIC Digest*. Washington, DC: Office of Educational Research and Improvement & U.S. Department of Education. (ERIC Document Reproduction Service No. ED 421 281)
   These authors show how you can help learners take ownership of their learning by allowing them some voice in class activities as well as their evaluation.
Beed, P. L., Hawkings, E. M., & Roller, C. M. (1991). Moving learners toward independence: The power of scaffolded instruction. *The Reading Teacher, 44*(9), 648–55.
   Discusses the constructivist concept of scaffolding and describes how it can be accomplished in numerous ways in teaching.
Borich, G., & Tombari, M. (1995). Educational psychology: A contemporary approach. New York: HarperCollins.
   A review of the research that provides the foundation for self-directed learning and cognitive learning strategies (Chapter 5).
*Cooney, B. (1982). *Miss Rumphius*. New York: Trumpet Club.
   To keep a promise to her grandfather, Miss Rumphius seeks to make the world a better place. (Can be used for Small Group Assessment Activity listed above or begin a discussion about sources of motivation.)
[1]Davis, B. A. (1994). Mathematics teaching: Moving from telling to listening. *Journal of Curriculum and Supervision, 9*(3), 267–83.
   Contrasts two teaching approaches to mathematics and notes the importance of how teachers listen to students. Reminds the reader that listening differs from hearing.

*Children's literature suitable for the Small Group Assessment Activity.

*dePaola, T. (1993). *Strega Nona meets her match*. New York: Scholastic.

Big Anthony goes to work for Strega Nona's competition and unwittingly saves the day.

Duffy, G., Roehler, L., & Herrmann, B. (1988). Modeling mental processes helps poor readers become strategic readers. *The Reading Teacher, 41*(8), 762–7.

A practical application of metacognitive strategies in an elementary classroom.

Ediger, M. (1994, Fall). Pupils learn on their own in science. *Science Activities, 31*(3), 15–6.

Discusses ways teachers can set up an environment which encourages effective incidental learning of science concepts.

Edwards, C. H. (1997). Promoting student inquiry. *The Science Teacher, 6*(7) 18–21.

Suggests that students need help in generating good questions, which then become the basis for strong science inquiry experiences.

Fisher, B. (1994). Workshop time: Generating curriculum. *Teaching Pre K–8, 25*(2), 63–5.

A primary grade teacher describes ways she encourages her students to generate their own curriculum during workshop time.

Greenwood, S. C. (1995). Learning contracts and transaction: A natural marriage in the middle. *Language Arts, 72*(2), 88–96.

Suggests that using learning contracts with middle school students can help build community as it builds language arts skill.

Kay, S. (1994). From theory to practice—Promoting problem-finding behavior in children. *Roeper Review, 16*(3), 195–7.

The author describes a discovery unit designed to help 67 gifted children in grades 3–6 develop problem-solving behaviors. Results suggest that teachers should instruct and help students practice problem-finding skills at the elementary level.

Meltzer, L. J., Roditi, B. N., Haynes, D. P., Biddle, K. R., Paster, M., & Taber, S. E. (1996). *Strategies for success: Classroom teaching techniques for students with learning problems.* Austin, TX: Pro-ed.

Describes ways to teach late elementary, middle, and high school students to use particular strategies to enhance their studying effectiveness. Also offers five case studies so readers can see the application of the strategies in the lives of students.

Miholic, V. (1994). An inventory to pique students' metacognitive awareness of reading strategies. *Journal of Reading, 38*(2), 84–6.

Provides a short questionnaire students can complete (from junior high through college age) to become more aware of metacognitive reading strategies they use and may want to learn.

Palincsar, A., & Brown, A. (1989). Classroom dialogues to promote self-regulated comprehension. In J. Brophy (Ed.), *Advances in research on teaching,* (Vol. 1, pp. 35–71). Greenwich, CT: JAI Press.

The authors demonstrate how modeling and social dialogue in the classroom can contribute to student self-inquiry skills through reciprocal teaching.

Peace, N., Feunteun, T., & Walker, M. (1997). Investigation of the great pyramid of giza. *Mathematics in School, 26*(1), 6–8.

Presents some interesting experimental results and encourages response. Demonstrates nicely the role discovery learning can play in students' lives.

Pressley, M., Borkowski, J., & Schneider, W. (1987). Good strategy users coordinate metacognition, strategy use, and knowledge. In R. Vasta & G. Whitehurst (Eds.), *Annals of child development* (Vol. 4, pp. 89–130). Greenwich, CT: JAI Press.

How metacognitive techniques can be combined with other effective teaching methods to increase independent thinking and problem solving.

Rekrut, M. D. (1999). Using the Internet in classroom instruction: A primer for teachers. *Journal of Adolescent & Adult Literacy, 42*(7), 546–57.

This author shows how to use the Internet to present metacognitive strategies and mental modeling to help students organize their thinking and become independent learners.

Roehler, L., & Duffy, G. (1987). Why are some teachers better explainers than others? *Journal of Education for Teaching, 12*(3), 273–84.

Presents some techniques for achieving lesson clarity in which learners are encouraged to take responsibility for their own learning.

Rohrkemper, M., & Corno, L. (1988). Success and failure on classroom tasks: Adaptive learning and classroom teaching. *The Elementary School Journal, 88*(3), 298–312.

The authors discuss techniques by which learners can adapt classroom tasks to their individual learning styles to control their own learning.

* San Souci, R. D. (1989). *The boy and the ghost.* New York: Trumpet Club.

A young boy braves a haunted mansion to help his family financially.

Spires, H. A., & Stone, P. D. (1989). The Directed Notetaking Activity: A self-questioning approach. *Journal of Reading, 33*(1), 36–9.

Suggests that students may benefit less from note-taking than they should because they have not brought much of the process to a conscious level. Offers a step-by-step guide for helping students take better notes and make more use of them for learning.

*Van Allsburg, C. (1993). *The sweetest fig.* New York: Houghton Mifflin.

Monsieur Bibot's greed leads him to a surprising conclusion.

Wilson, R. A. (1997). The wonders of nature: Honoring children's ways of knowing. *Early Childhood News, 9*(2), 6–9, 16–9.

Notes that young children come to know their world through sensory means. This sensory means is increasingly deemphasized as students mature.

Suggests that a good curriculum for young (and even older) students includes the opportunity to sense the world and wonder about things.

*Children's literature suitable for the Small Group Assessment Activity.

ACTIVE LEARNING

RECIPROCAL TEACHING is a powerful strategy. Students in a small group use the skills of predicting, questioning, clarifying, and summarizing to interact with challenging material. Through the use of these four skills, the students learn how to set purposes for reading, how to critically evaluate and monitor themselves, and how to find the main idea in the text. The teacher initially models the interactive dialogue, with the students following the teacher's example, and engaging in the same activities.

This strategy is designed to help students focus on four specific comprehension strategies and actively use them in participating in and leading class discussions. It includes a teacher modeling component, and gradually, the teacher fades from control as students take over the discussion themselves.

Planning for a reciprocal teaching lesson has two phases. First, become familiar with text selection by following this five-step procedure.

1. Identify which text segments will be used to demonstrate the four comprehension strategies.
2 Identify salient questions in the selection and generate additional questions about the material.
3. Generate possible predictions about each text segment.
4. Underline summarizing sentences and generate possible summaries for each text segment.
5. Circle difficult vocabulary or concepts.

Second, make two diagnostic decisions about the students who will participate.

1. Decide what strategies the students already use when reading and what is needed to help them learn from the text.
2. Evaluate the students' abilities to generate text questions, summarize, predict, clarify, and decide what kind of support they will need to participate in and eventually lead each of these activities.

Instructional Procedure for Reciprocal Teaching Strategy

1. When reciprocal teaching is first introduced, the teacher and the students should discuss why the text may be difficult to understand, why strategies are important to help with the understanding and studying of the text and how reciprocal teaching will help the students monitor themselves as they read. Next, the students should be given an overall description of reciprocal teaching, and an explanation of the four strategies to be used. The explanations should include these four major comprehension strategies:

   Summarizing—this gives the student the opportunity to identify and integrate the most important information in the text. The students begin by summarizing sentences, and with time and practice, progress to summarizing paragraphs and passages.

   Question Generating—the students are deciding which information is important enough to provide the substance for a question. They can teach themselves to ask questions in which they must infer and apply new information from the text.

   Clarifying—this skill is particularly helpful to those students who have trouble with comprehension. They come to realize that various factors, such as new vocabulary, unclear referent words, or difficult concepts, may make a text very hard to understand. Once they are taught to be alert to these factors, they can take the necessary steps to restore meaning.

   Predicting—by using prediction, the students must activate their background knowledge, and have a purpose set for reading. They are then called upon to set a hypothesis about what the author will discuss next in the text. Reading to prove or disprove their hypothesis becomes a new purpose for reading. The students also learn that text structures provide clues as to what might happen next, through the use of headings, subheadings, and questions imbedded in the text.

2. The students should be given one day of practice for each of the four skills. For example, the students may practice summarization by summarizing their favorite movies or television shows. They then use the text to identify the main ideas in sentences, paragraphs, and eventually passages. The same type of instruction should be repeated for all of the skills.

3. After the students have been introduced to each of the skills, the teacher begins to introduce the students to the actual dialogue. On the first day of instruction, the teacher models reciprocal teaching. It is important that he or she calls on every student to participate at some level.

4. As the students become more familiar with the procedure, the teacher turns over the responsibility for the dialogue to them. He or she then becomes a coach, and provides the students with evaluative information, prompting them to more and higher levels of participation.

Source: "Collaborative Research and Development of Reciprocal Teaching," by A. S. Palincsar, K. Ransom, and S. Derber in *Educational Leadership* (pp. 37-40). December 1988/January 1989 Vol. 6, no. 4. Alexandria, VA: Association for Supervision and Curriculum Development. 1989 ASCD. Reprinted by permission. All rights reserved.

SONG-WRITING

Write a song to be sung to the tune "Are You Sleeping" by completing the following form:

Who? (4 syllables)	
Repeat (same 4 syllables)	
_____ Where was the character or idea at the beginning? (3 syllables)	_____ Where at the end? (3 syllables)
(1) _____ (3) _____ Think of 4 -ing words that describe this thing (12 syllables)	(2) _____ (4) _____
_____ Summarize the main idea (3 syllables)	_____ Repeat summary or add more summation (3 syllables)

Here's an example for the story of the *Three Little Pigs*:

> **Big, mean wolfie: Big, mean wolfie**
> **At the door: In the pot**
> **Huffing, puffing, falling, stewing,**
> **In the pot—**
> **Tough you're not!**

Source: Polette, N. (1991). *Whole language in action.* Paper presented at the regular meeting of the Central Utah Reading Council, Orem, UT. Nancy can be contacted through the company Book Lures at: P. O. Box 9450, O'Fallon, MO 63366, telephone (800) 444-9450.

Study Guide: Chapter 8

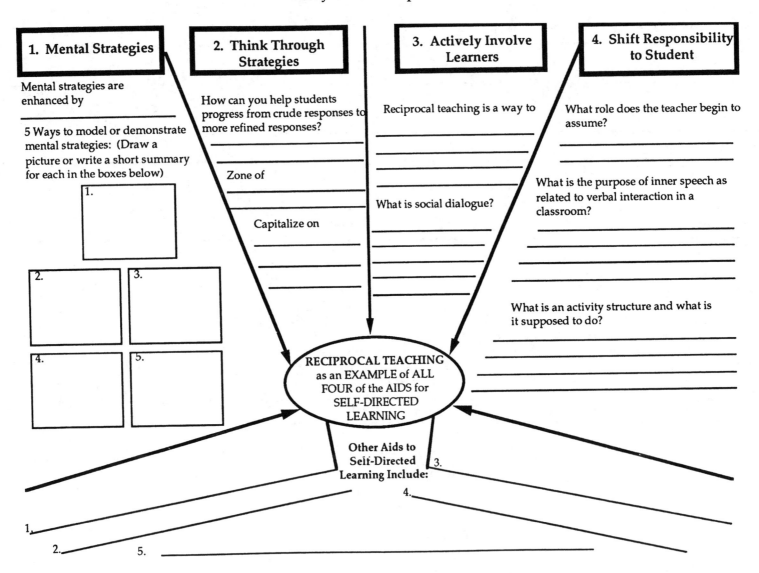

1. Mental Strategies

Mental strategies are enhanced by
_____

5 Ways to model or demonstrate mental strategies: (Draw a picture or write a short summary for each in the boxes below)

1.

2.   3.

4.   5.

2. Think Through Strategies

How can you help students progress from crude responses to more refined responses?
_____
_____

Zone of
_____
_____

Capitalize on
_____
_____
_____
_____
_____

3. Actively Involve Learners

Reciprocal teaching is a way to
_____
_____
_____
_____

What is social dialogue?
_____
_____
_____
_____

4. Shift Responsibility to Student

What role does the teacher begin to assume?
_____
_____
_____

What is the purpose of inner speech as related to verbal interaction in a classroom?
_____
_____
_____

What is an activity structure and what is it supposed to do?
_____
_____
_____
_____
_____

RECIPROCAL TEACHING as an EXAMPLE of ALL FOUR of the AIDS for SELF-DIRECTED LEARNING

Other Aids to Self-Directed Learning Include:

1._____

2._____   5. _____

3. _____

4. _____

BRIDGES

Chapter 9
Cooperative Learning
and the Collaborative Process

Chapter 9	A. *Personal, Dialogue, or Buddy Journals*	B. *Self-Directed Study Activities*	C. *Cooperative & Collaborative Ideas*	D. *Whole Class*
Introducing the Content	1. **REFLECT** on your experiences in working on projects in pairs or in groups. What was good? What was bad? What might you change? Why?	1. Think about yourself and **COMPLETE THE FOLLOWING STATEMENT:** "When it comes to working in groups, I prefer _____ because _____." **ELABORATE** on your ideas. How might your personal preferences relate to your teaching style and choices?	1. Working in pairs, **ADDRESS** the following questions: What does it mean to collaborate? To cooperate? **COMPLETE THE MOVEMENT ACTIVITY** (p. 75) to illustrate the two concepts. What implications do you see for teaching regarding the two ideas?	1. **MAKE TWO COLUMNS** on a chalkboard or overhead transparency. Head one column with the word "collaborative" and the other column with the word "cooperative." **BRAINSTORM** meanings for the two terms and **COMPARE** and **CONTRAST** them.

Chapter 9 continued	A. *Personal, Dialogue, or Buddy Journals*	B. *Self-Directed Study Activities*	C. *Cooperative & Collaborative Ideas*	D. *Whole Class*
Assimilating/ Reviewing the Content	2. How does the concept of structure relate to learners? Do learners "need" a structure? Structure in what? How much? 3. How do you feel about the statement "2 heads are better than one"? Is it true in learning? Are 2 or more heads ever less helpful? When?	2. **SKIM** work by Slavin (p. 74) and **CHOOSE** a cooperative learning technique you like. **CRITIQUE** it, identifying its strengths, weaknesses, and best applications. **PRESENT** and "sell" this strategy to your peers, or **TEST IT OUT** in a teaching situation (if you are tutoring, etc.). What did you discover? 3. What would you **GUESS** are some of the most common errors teachers make in trying to implement cooperative learning strategies? How might a teacher avoid some of these errors?	2. **USE A JIGSAW FORMAT** (p. 76) to learn about the cooperative strategies summarized in this guide (or others which your instructor suggests).	2. If you have used collaborative or cooperative groups in the class, spend a few minutes **DISCUSSING** how these groups have worked and what strengths and weaknesses students have seen in their use. If you have not used these groups, ask students to **SHARE EXPERIENCES** from classes or courses where they have done so. **FOCUS** especially on what works well within such groups and what purposes are best achieved through collaborative and cooperative grouping.

Chapter 9: Checking Your Understanding

True or False:

1. _____ An ideal group size for cooperative groups is 2–3 so students all have opportunity to speak and be heard.
2. _____ Cooperative learning activities are less appropriate for field-dependent learners because they prefer to work by themselves and compete.
3. _____ Cooperative learning is an instructional approach designed to help students think for themselves and define their own attitudes and values through interaction with others.
4. _____ If time is short, it is better to focus on group projects rather than debriefing about activities, since debriefing is less important to the cooperative process than other stages.
5. _____ Debriefing involves openly talking about how groups functioned in a particular cooperative task and considering ways that groups might improve their interactions.
6. _____ One of the major drawbacks in using cooperative learning is the difficulty of assigning grades to the work.
7. _____ In culturally diverse classrooms, the best instructional choice is to be structured and direct so that students know what is expected and can avoid uncomfortable confrontations with peers.
8. _____ Cooperative learning activities completed in teams encourage collaborative skills, self-esteem and achievement of individual learners.
9. _____ One goal of cooperative learning is for students to see and experience prosocial behavior.

Multiple Choice:

10. _____ Which of the following steps is not part of establishing a cooperative learning activity?
    a. Structuring the task
    b. Monitoring group performance
    c. Debriefing
    d. Maintaining full control of learning activities

11. _____ Which of the cooperative group role descriptions below is incorrect?
    a. summarizer—paraphrases and repeats back to the group major conclusions for agreement
    b. checker—checks statements and conclusions for accuracy, especially at the end of a task before presentation
    c. researcher—provides critical information for the group during the work
    d. recorder—records minutes of the group's actions that may be useful for later whole-class debriefing

1. F   2. F   3. T   4. F   5. T   6. F   7. F   8. T   9. T   10. d   11. d

Chapter 9: Performance Assessment Ideas		
Individual	*Small Group*	*Whole Class*
1. **WRITE** about several ways you could assign roles within cooperative groups of students. Include advantages and disadvantages of each choice. 2. **OBSERVE** a lesson where cooperative or collaborative approaches are being used. **INTERVIEW** a student (with the teacher's and student's permission) for his or her perspective. **WRITE** a short summary of your experience.	1. **BRAINSTORM** 2–3 problems that might occur in cooperative or collaborative settings. **WRITE** a short scenario of each and include how you might solve each difficulty. 2. **INTERVIEW** a teacher who uses cooperative or collaborative grouping strategies regarding major advantages and disadvantages of these approaches. **WRITE** a brief summary of your experience.	1. **DISCUSS** as a class what strengths and weaknesses your group exhibits with respect to cooperation and collaboration. **CHOOSE** an area in which to improve and **BRAINSTORM** possible alternatives. **RESOLVE** as a class to implement an alternative and **EVALUATE** your progress in a week or two.

CHILDREN'S LITERATURE CONNECTION

Cowen-Fletcher, J. (1994). *It takes a village*. New York: Scholastic.
    Yemi learns that watching her little brother involves the whole village.
Lionni, L. (1964). *Tico and the golden wings*. New York: Scholastic.
    Golden Bird gives away all his feathers and becomes black in color like his friends. Discussion could center on questions such as: Do we have to look the same to belong? Are we the same even if we appear to be on the outside?
Lionni, L. (1969). *Alexander and the wind-up mouse*. New York: Dragonfly Books.
    Alexander wants to be a wind-up mouse like Willy until he learns of the toy's imminent fate. What he learns next is the joy of caring for another and realizing that the grass isn't always greener on the other side.
Lionni, L. (1975). *A color of his own*. New York: Scholastic.
    A chameleon learns it's more fun to share.
Lionni, L. (1985). *It's mine!* New York: Scholastic.
    The quarrelsome frogs learn it's more rewarding to share than to compete.
Muntean, M. (1980). *If I lived alone*. New York: Western Publishing Co.
    While the author muses how many advantages there are in living alone, she concludes that we all need each other.
Numeroff, L. (1997). *The chicken sisters*. New York: Scholastic.
    Community members are irritated by the chicken sisters, until they see the sisters' "talents" in a new light.

Pfister, M. (1992). *The rainbow fish*. New York: North-South Books.

The rainbow fish finds joy in sharing her glittery scales. While this story may offer a positive view of sharing/collaborating, other discussion may center on whether one should alter oneself to gain acceptance of the group—and if so, to what degree.

SUGGESTED READINGS

Artzt, A. F. (1994). Integrating writing and cooperative learning in the mathematics class. *The Mathematics Teacher, 87*(2), 80–5.

The author describes activities used in teacher preparation classes which can be applied to teaching writing, mathematics, and cooperative learning in other grades.

Boyd, S. L., & Tompkins, R. S. (1992). Preparing preservice teachers to implement cooperative learning successfully. *Contemporary Education, 63*(3), 203–6.

Reminds the reader that cooperative learning is not an easy strategy to implement, especially in certain settings.

Brent, R., & Anderson, P. (1993). Developing children's classroom listening strategies. *The Reading Teacher, 47*(2), 122–6.

Notes that students need to become good listeners to facilitate learning and communication. Suggests that teachers should model good listening, teach lessons in listening, and provide meaningful reasons for students to listen.

Bruffee, K. R. (1995). Sharing our toys. *Change, 27*(1), 12–8.

Although aimed at university teachers and administrators, this article discusses some differences between cooperative and collaborative learning as well as the processes required to help people work successfully in groups.

Irvine, J., & York, D. (2001). Learning Styles and Culturally Diverse Students: A Literature Review. In J. Banks & C. Banks (Eds.), *Handbook of research on multicultural education* (pp. 484–97). San Francisco: Jossey-Bass.

From a review of the literature, Irvine and York identify characteristics of students who need more or less structure to maximize their opportunity to learn. The implications of field independence and field dependence for cooperative learning are related to students' need for structure.

Johnson, D., & Johnson, R. (1991). *Learning together and alone* (3rd ed.). Upper Saddle River, NJ: Merrill/Prentice Hall.

One of the most popular and complete texts on cooperative learning, written especially for the beginning teacher.

Kagan, S. (1995). Group grades miss the mark. *Educational Leadership, 53*(8), 68–71.

Explains that teachers should never give group grades for cooperative learning activities. Offers grading ideas and alternatives.

Kletzien, S. B., & Baloche, L. (1994). The shifting muffled sound of the pick: Facilitating student-to-student discussion. *Journal of Reading, 37*(7), 540–5.

Offers ideas on structuring discussion activities within cooperative learning settings as well as in one-on-one interactions.

Lookatch, R. P. (1996). Collaborative learning and multimedia: Are two heads still better than one? *Techtrends, 41*(4), 27–31.

Discusses issues for consideration when using computers and collaborative learning strategies.

Marzano, R., Pickering, J., & Pollock, J. (2001). *Classroom instruction that works: Research-based strategies for increasing student achievement.* Alexandria, VA: Association for Supervision and Curriculum Development.

In this booklet, the authors show how you can improve students' ability to work with others and acquire social awareness to prepare them to reason and perform in an adult world.

Mevarech, Z. R., & Susak, Z. (1993). Effects of learning with cooperative-mastery method on elementary students. *Journal of Educational Research, 86*(4), 197–205.

In an interesting study, the authors combine questioning strategies with collaborative learning.

Mickel, V. L. (1993). Using cooperative learning in teaching content reading. *Journal of Reading, 36*(8), 659–60

Describes a specific strategy for having cooperative groups read new content area material.

Poindexter, C. (1995). Applying effective reading techniques in content area classes. *Reading Horizons, 35*(3), 244–9.

Suggests ways that cooperative techniques can be used effectively with older students.

Slavin, R. (1990). *Cooperative learning: Theory, research and practice.* Upper Saddle River, NJ: Merrill/Prentice Hall.

A thorough review of the uses and benefits of cooperative learning—with important ideas for implementing cooperative learning in your classroom.

Slavin, R. (1991). Are cooperative learning and untracking harmful to the gifted? *Educational Leadership, 48,* 68–71.

An important discussion of how cooperative learning can be of benefit in the heterogeneously grouped classroom.

Slavin, R. (1993). *Student team learning: An overview and practical guide.* Washington, DC: National Education Association.

A concise and practical discussion of how to implement four cooperative learning activities in the classroom.

Smith, L. J., & Smith, D. L. (1994). The discussion process: A simulation. *Journal of Reading, 37*(7), 582–5.

Describes how to plan and implement a discussion simulation as a way to instruct students to achieve better discussions.

Vermette, P. (1994, September). The right start for cooperative learning. *Education Digest,* 35–8.

Describes four traps to avoid in first using cooperative learning.

Wiencek, J., & Jones J. P. (1994). From teacher-led to peer discussions about literature: Suggestions for making the shift. *Language Arts, 71*(7), 488–98.

Addresses several questions teachers raise as they shift from teacher-led to student-led discussions.

Wood, K., & Jones, J. P. (1994). Integrating collaborative learning across the curriculum. *Middle School Journal, 25*(3), 19–23.

Offers a number of examples for using collaborative learning approaches within an integrated curriculum.

Zajac, R. J., & Hartup, W. W. (1997). Friends as coworkers: Research review and classroom implications. *The Elementary School Journal, 98*(1), 3–13.

Makes the point that student learning is usually enhanced when students are allowed to work with friends—peers they like and feel comfortable with.

ACTIVE LEARNING

MOVEMENT ACTIVITY

Students work in pairs. One is the sculptor, the other is to be "sculpted." The sculptor fashions the material into a statue depicting an emotion or event. At a signal from the instructor, sculptors stop and sculptures "freeze." Sculptors move about the room and inspect the sculptures, guessing at the possible messages. Pairs can then trade roles. Students can then compare the differences in working alone as a sculptor and sculpting with a partner. (Teachers may play soft background music during "sculpting" to enhance the artistic mood of the experience.)

COOPERATIVE LEARNING

A. **Jigsaw**
   Roles: Recorder, timer, spokesman, encourages, monitor (of interaction), reader
   1. Number each item from 1–4.
   2. Have all the 1s meet in a given area to read and discuss specific information.
   3. Do the same with 2–4.
   4. After a given amount of time, have numbered members return to their "home" teams to share the knowledge gained in each area.

B. **Numbered Heads Together**
   1. Have students number off within groups, so that each student is a 1, 2, 3, or 4.

   2. Ask a high-consensus question, such as "When did Columbus sail?"
   3. Tell the students to put their heads together to make sure everyone on the team knows the answer.
   4. Call a number (1, 2, 3, or 4) and have all the students with that number share their answers (through writing on the chalkboard, writing on a paper and holding it up, etc.).
   5. Continue with increasingly difficult questions. Keep "score" if so desired.

C. **Roundtable**
   1. Ask a question with many possible answers.
   2. Have students in groups make a list of all of their answers, with each person writing an answer on the paper and passing it to the next person.

   3. The paper goes around the table until time is called, and then answers are shared and discussed.

   An interesting variation of **Roundtable** is to send around four papers at a time so each person is always writing—or students can pass papers back and forth in pairs and when time is called, share their paper with the other pair in their group.

D. **Roundrobin (Oral counterpart of Roundtable)**

   1. Ask a question with many possible answers.

   2. Have each student take a turn (round robin reading style) providing an answer to the question.

   3. When time is called, someone in the group summarizes ideas from the group.

E. **Team Word-Webbing**

   1. Give each student a different color pen or marker and give the team one large poster paper, butcher paper, etc.

   2. Have students write the main concept of your lesson in the center of the paper.

   3. Have students think of words to add in roundtable style to the web.

   4. Place webs at the front of the room and discuss interesting insights.

   This can be completed before a lesson begins, and again at its conclusion to enhance connections and ideas. It can be part of a discussion starter, or simply the concluding activity to "bring together" ideas.

Sources: This material has been adapted from the following book with permission from Kagan Publishing & Professional Development: Kagan, Spencer. *Cooperative Learning.* San Clemente, CA: Resources For Teachers, 1994. Templeton, Shane, *Teaching the Integrated Language Arts.* Copyright (©) 1991 by Houghton Mifflin Company. Reprinted with permission.
1(800) 993-2667; www.KaganOnline.com/.
(Numbered Heads Together, Kagan, 1994)

BRIDGES

Chapter 10
Classroom Management

Chapter 10	A. *Personal, Dialogue, or Buddy Journals*	B. *Self-Directed Study Activities*	C. *Cooperative & Collaborative Ideas*	D. *Whole Class*
Introducing the Content	1. **THINK BACK** to teachers you consider competent or less competent. What were the differences? What cued you as to their abilities? 2. Do you ever act differently in one class than another? Why? Would you be embarrassed if your favorite teacher watched how you acted in your least favorite class? Why?	1. **MAP** your ideal classroom and **SUMMARIZE** your reasons for the arrangement of items. 2. **READ** the **CAR STORY** in the **ACTIVE LEARNING** section (p. 83). What insights do you gain from considering this story in relation to classroom management? In relation to coming to know and understand your students?	1. Form groups or pairs according to the grade level and setting in which you hope to teach and **BRAINSTORM** a set of rules for that grade. **SHARE** memories of experiences/rules you found personally effective before creating the list. 2. **BRAINSTORM** some ideas for smooth transitions between activities.	1. Have a clear opening and closing today and **POINT THEM OUT.** 2. Have students **SHARE** their "first day" of teaching fears. **SHARE** the **PORCUPINE STORY** (p. 83) and provide some concrete suggestions for the first day of class.

Chapter 10 continued	A. Personal, Dialogue, or Buddy Journals	B. Self-Directed Study Activities	C. Cooperative & Collaborative Ideas	D. Whole Class
Assimilating/ Reviewing the Content	3. **COMPARE AND CONTRAST** the words "classroom control" and "classroom management." What does each encompass with respect to an educational philosophy? What does each instill or preclude?	3. **REVIEW** the five types of social power. Where do you think you have strengths? **READ** in an area you'd like to strengthen and **SET A CONCRETE GOAL** for a way to grow there. 4. How do you plan to manage your classroom? What kind of classroom climate do you hope to create? Why? What are some steps you'll take to do this? Should you allow other climates? Why or why not?	3. **BRAINSTORM** some good openings and closings for a particular lesson. Remember to consider lively poetry, etc. as good attention-getters (as noted in Chapter 4). 4. **DISCUSS** with a partner the following question: Have you been part of a group that successfully achieved all four stages of development? **REFLECT** on how and why that happened and the implications from that experience for you as a teacher.* 5. **WRITE** a letter for parents that reflects your classroom management plan and intended class rules. **READ** it to a partner/group and make revisions.	3. **REFLECT** with students on effective and ineffective management strategies they have experienced over the years. **LINK** the discussion back to Chapter 1 engagement ideas: Discipline problems may occur because students are not engaged.

*Note: Because students learned about 5 different cooperative grouping strategies in Chapter 9 (if you completed that activity), vary the grouping strategies here. Debrief not only on the activity content, but on how the group felt about the strategy.

Chapter 10: Checking Your Understanding

True or False:

1. _____ Teachers can do very little to influence classroom norms.
2. _____ The physical arrangement of a classroom contributes little to the overall social climate.
3. _____ Referent power is the kind of influence a teacher gains with students when they feel their teacher is trustworthy, fair, and concerned about them as individuals.
4. _____ If group members rebel against group norms, it is a sure sign that the norms were improperly established.
5. _____ One of the best ways to communicate "withitness" is through use of eye contact.
6. _____ Reward power is so strong that it eradicates the value of any other kind of teacher power in the classroom.
7. _____ It is helpful to display a listing of prior assignments somewhere in the classroom for students who miss class or need to make up work for some reason.
8. _____ Coercive power is the most effective type of social power teachers can use to establish a healthy and productive classroom environment.
9. _____ Competitive activities have little value in establishing or maintaining an effective classroom climate and should thus be avoided.
10. _____ Even if a lesson has gone well, closure is still important to help students remember what was learned and place it in perspective.

Multiple Choice:

11. _____ Successful groups tend to pass through which of the following series of stages?
    a. Forming (acceptance); Storming (resolving concerns about shared influence); Norming (resolving concerns about work); Performing (resolving concerns about freedom, control, self-regulation)
    b. Forming (meeting one another); Storming (engaging in natural conflict); Norming (comparing the class against others); Performing (demonstrating achievement)
12. _____ Which of the following are the most common reasons teachers experience difficulty in making transitions from one activity to another (Mark all that apply)
    a. Learners are overly anxious to perform the next activity
    b. Learners are still working on the previous activity and are not ready to move to the next activity
    c. Learners have not been taught what to do during the transition
    d. Each transition is unique to its setting so learners must approach every one as a new experience

| 1. F | 2. F | 3. T | 4. F | 5. T | 6. F |
| 7. T | 8. F | 9. F | 10. T | 11. a | 12. b, c |

79

Chapter 10: Performance Assessment Ideas		
Individual	*Small Group*	*Whole Class*
1. **RESPOND** to the **ASSESSMENT ACTIVITY** (p. 84). 2. Use the **COOPERATIVE/ COLLABORATIVE LEARNING PLANNING SHEET** (p. 85) to think through a cooperative/collaborative activity you would like to teach. Complete the activity and reflect on its success as well as the helpfulness of the planning sheet. 3. According to the article below,[1] prospective teachers should try science strategies to build teaching confidence. How might (or does) this occur in your teacher preparation program? **SUMMARIZE** your ideas and **SUGGEST** possible changes to improve the experience.	1. **READ** the **GENERAL GUIDELINES FOR BEGINNING TEACHERS** (p. 86) and **RESPOND** to them. Are there any guidelines you would alter? Any you would add? Why or why not? **SUPPORT** your ideas from your class text and other significant sources. 2. Moeller[2] suggests that academic success builds self-esteem rather than self-esteem building academic success. In some ways, this resembles the question of whether the chicken or the egg came first. **WHAT** do you think? Which comes first—academic success or self-esteem? **WHY** do you think so? How can you **DEFEND** your views? How might these views **TRANSLATE** into teaching practices?	1. **BRAINSTORM** how your group functions according to the stage descriptions in the text. In what areas is the group strong? In what areas might it improve?

CHILDREN'S LITERATURE CONNECTION

Arnold, T. (1993). *Green Wilma*. New York: Scholastic.
    Wilma wakes up green and behaves like a frog all day. Surprise ending can spark discussion about whether Wilma was misbehaving (and whether students are sometimes "being themselves" rather than breaking rules). Unfortunately, real classroom challenges aren't a dream from which we awake.
Krauss, R. (1945). *The carrot seed*. New York: Scholastic.
    In this tried and true favorite, a little boy maintains his faith and patient care of a carrot seed until it produces an incredible harvest. In the same way, classroom management takes consistent effort and attention, and often grows from small seeds of routine and positive interaction. Further, the fact that the little boy persevered in his efforts to grow a carrot in spite of discouraging feedback may have stemmed partly from the fact of ownership: the carrot belonged to HIM. In like manner, classroom policies in which students have a voice and stake are more likely to succeed.

Marshall, J. (1977). *Miss Nelson is missing!* New York: Scholastic.

    Unable to manage her unruly class, Miss Nelson is replaced by mean Viola Swamp.

Marshall, J. (1984). *The Cut-Ups.* New York: Trumpet Club.

    See entry immediately below.

Marshall, J. (1987). *The Cut-Ups cut loose.* New York: Trumpet Club.

    How would you handle these students? What do Sister Aloysius and La Mar J. Spurgle do that works/doesn't work? How do you feel about the stereotyping of the characters? How does stereotyping affect behavior?

Murphy, J. (1986). *Five minutes' peace.* New York: Scholastic.

    Mrs. Large just wants five minutes' peace from her children—being with children is a full-time job (whether at home or at school).

Rathman, P. (1991). *Ruby the copycat.* New York: Scholastic.

    Ruby moves to a new school and copies everything from others—until a wise teacher helps her see her own talents. Highlights the role of sensitivity in dealing with apparent misbehaviors.

Teague, M. (1987). *Baby tamer.* New York: Scholastic.

    Babysitter Amanda doesn't become distressed when the children try all their best pranks. What's her secret? Can it help teachers?

SUGGESTED READINGS

Adkins, A., & Rogers, D. (1994). "We don't have any rules. We have guidelines." *Teaching Education, 6*(10), 145–8.

    Two experienced third grade teachers reflect on how they manage their classrooms.

Almeida, D. A. (1995, September). Behavior management and "The Five C's." *Teaching K–8,* 88–9.

    Offers a five-step plan for helping students to learn appropriate behavior.

Borich, G. (1993). *Clearly outstanding: Making each day count in your classroom.* Boston: Allyn & Bacon.

    Through the eyes and ears of three teachers, Angela, Kurt, and Sheila, this book shows how teachers can establish a positive relationship with their class and as a result improve the effectiveness of their teaching. It also illustrates how the beginning teacher grows professionally and personally from the challenges presented by teaching groups of learners.

Bowers, C. A., & Flinders, D. J. (1990). *Responsive teaching: An ecological approach to patterns of language, culture, and thought.* New York: Teachers College Press.

    An original and thoughtful analysis of how cultural patterns of thought and language affect a teacher's classroom management decisions.

Chambers, L. (1994). What makes a student improve? *Teaching Education, 6*(1), 9–19.

    An experienced, 7th grade world history teacher reflects on and researches about students' motivation. Discovers that teacher influence is a big factor, especially when the teacher is interested in how students learn.

Charles, C. M. (1992). *Building classroom discipline: From models to practice* (3rd ed.). New York: Longman.

    A comprehensive survey of the major theoretical approaches to classroom discipline, it presents helpful suggestions for developing your own personalized system of classroom management.

Compton-Lilly, C. (2000). "Staying on Children": Challenging stereotypes about urban parents. *Language Arts, 77*(5), 420–7.

    This author presents convincing arguments that teachers of different cultures often interpret disruptive behaviors of children differently.

Elberfeld, R. L. (1994, October). Bits of wisdom you just can't teach without. *Teaching K–8*, 66–7.
> *Lighthearted look at some things to remember at the year's beginning combined with some helpful ideas.*

Elements of an effective discipline strategy. (1995/1996, Winter). *American Educator*, 24–7.
> *Written by the staff of the American Federation of Teachers, this article highlights the need for clear discipline policies not only at the classroom level, but beyond.*

Emmer, E., Evertson, C., & Worsham, M. (2003). *Classroom management for secondary teachers*. New York: Longman.
> *Presents detailed, step-by-step activities and principles for planning and organizing secondary classrooms. The recommendations are derived from observations of the best practices of effective teachers.*

[1]Enochs, L. G., Scharmann, L. G., & Riggs, I. M. (1995). The relationship of pupil control to preservice elementary science teacher self-efficacy and outcome expectancy. *Science Education, 79*(1), 63–75.
> *Preservice teachers who expected to succeed at teaching science did—authors conclude that prospective teachers should be actively involved in teaching experience to build their confidence. Students should try strategies during early field experience.*

Evertson, C., Emmer, E., & Worsham, M. (2003). *Classroom management for elementary teachers*. New York: Longman.
> *Presents detailed, step-by-step activities and principles for planning and organizing elementary classrooms. The recommendations are derived from observations of the best practices of effective teachers.*

Fuhler, C. J. (1994). Response journals: Just one more time with feeling. *Journal of Reading, 37*(5), 400–5.
> *Discusses how she extended journals form her eighth grade classroom to involve the parents with positive results.*

Glasser, William. (1998b). *The quality school: Managing students without coercion* (Rev. ed.). New York: HarperPerennial.
> *Among other important classroom management topics, Glasser urges teachers to have class discussions centering around group conflict resolution and tells how they can accomplish this in the classroom.*

Greenwood, S. C. (1995). Learning contracts and transaction: A natural marriage in the middle. *Language Arts, 72*(2), 88–96.
> *Suggests that using learning contracts with middle school students can help build community as it builds language arts skill.*

Howe, A. C. (1994, Spring). How do you manage? *Science Activities, 31*(1), 11–3.
> *Suggests that teachers need to think through managing hands-on science activities well before class time to ensure success.*

Jones, V. F., & Jones, L. S. (1990). *Comprehensive classroom management* (3rd ed.). Boston: Allyn & Bacon.
> *Presents a detailed comprehensive discussion of the classroom management tradition. It offers many practical suggestions to both elementary and secondary school teachers on how to promote positive behavior.*

Kilgore, T. L., & Rubin, L. S. (1995). Collaboration for classroom behavior problems: Why it's difficult and how it can be implemented. *Teacher Education and Practice, 11*(1), 28–41.

Letts, N. (1994, August/September). Building classroom unity. *Teaching K–8*, 106–7.
> *Short piece with numerous examples of ways to involve students in building a sense of community and establishing group norms.*

[2]Moeller, T. G. (1994). What research says about self-esteem and academic performance. *Education Digest*, 34–7.
> *Notes that it may be better to help students build self-esteem by succeeding academically, rather than to attempt to build self-esteem to engender academic success.*

Putnam, J. (1997). *Cooperative learning in diverse classrooms*. Upper Saddle River, NJ: Merrill/Prentice Hall.
> *Among other important classroom management topics, Putnam urges teachers to engage in activities during the first few weeks of school to help learners trust one another and feel as members of a group and tells how they can accomplish this in the classroom.*

Savage, T. (1999). *Teaching self-control through management and discipline*. Boston: Allyn & Bacon.

This author presents an up-to-date classroom management text that emphasizes the prevention of classroom management problems and the student's own responsibility for managing their behavior—and techniques for doing so.

Schmuck, R., & Schmuck, P. (2001). *Group processes in the classroom* (8th ed.). Boston: McGraw-Hill.

Social psychologists, such as Patricia and Richard Schmuck, believe that the most effective learning involves being a member of a group. These authors show how you can use cooperative grouping and group processes to enhance learning, develop trust, and bestow the feeling that each learner is a valued member of a group.

Schwartz, W. (1998). The identity of development of multiracial youth. *ERIC/CUE Digest, Number 137.* New York: ERIC Clearinghouse on Urban Education.

This author discusses the compatibility of various classroom management techniques with the culture and background of the teacher.

Soleil, G. (1995). Understanding and identifying children with ADHD: First steps to effective intervention. *Policy Briefs:* Appalachia Educational Laboratory. (ERIC Document Reproduction Service No. ED 399 728)

Describes ADHD and includes a checklist for diagnosing students who may exhibit the disorder.

Weaver, R. L., II, Wenzlaff, S., & Catrell, H. W. (1993, October). How do students see master teachers? *Education Digest,* 12–5.

Traits students identified in several master teachers included having high standards/expectations and strong commitment to one's topic and job.

Wong, Harry K. (1998). *The first days of school: How to be an effective teacher.* Mountainview, CA: Harry K. Wong Publications.

If your first class day is like that of most teachers, it will include some or all of the emotions, problems, and activities this author writes about.

ACTIVE LEARNING

CAR STORY

The story is told of a man who, while driving his Mercedes at high speeds up a mountain road, was forced to slow down as a woman approached him from a blind curve—driving on HIS SIDE of the road.

Peeved, he swerved to miss her.

As the two cars passed, she called out, "Cow!"

Fuming, he took in her ample form, and responded, "Pig!"

Just then, he rounded the curve, only to crash headlong into a huge cow.

PORCUPINE STORY

Share this story with students to begin a discussion about how each person's behavior in a classroom affects the other students. Young students can later recall the discussion (along with class behavior rules) by simple reminders such as: "Remember the porcupines," or "Be sure you're not being a porcupine."

Philosopher Arthur Schopenhauer tells the following story which illustrates nicely the challenge in becoming close enough with others to survive and get along, and yet maintaining the "distance" of manners and propriety which provides a sense of safety:

"On a cold winter's day, a group of porcupines huddled together to stay warm and keep from freezing. But soon they felt one another's quills and moved apart. When the need for warmth brought them closer together again, their quills again forced them apart. They were driven back and forth at the mercy of their discomforts until they found the distance from one another that provided both a maximum of warmth and a minimum of pain.

"In human beings, the emptiness and monotony of the isolated self produces a need for society. This brings people together, but their many offensive qualities and intolerable faults drive them apart again. The optimum distance that they finally find and that permits them to coexist is embodied in politeness and good manners. Because of this distance between us, we can only partially satisfy our need for warmth, but at the same time, we are spared the stab of one another's quills."

Source: Schopenhauer, A. (1989). "Points to Ponder," *Reader's Digest,* 182.

Note: After sharing this story, you may want to return to the Gagné lesson plan and add a reminder about management challenges. Plan how you will assign and monitor work, interact with students, reach special needs students, etc.

ASSESSMENT ACTIVITY
John Klem believes that a stressed teacher can't get past himself or herself to motivate the students. He claims that teachers must deal with their personal stress before they can focus on the classroom. Given what you have read, experienced, and discussed (especially pertaining to this course) respond to Klem's comments. Conclude your response by attempting to refute the opposing view, supported with appropriate sources. If you disagree with Klem, reverse the steps listed above—first challenge his view, then seek to find strengths in his view, and finally, seek to refute those strengths, citing appropriate sources.

Cooperative/Collaborative Learning Planning Sheet

Think About	Description	My Plan
Group Size	4-member groups are ideal	
Group Assignment	What are you going to have them investigate or do?	
Room Arrangement	Can people interact easily?	
Materials: Plan & Distribute	What will they need to work with and how will you distribute it?	
Assigning Roles	Who will do what within each group: Recorder, Timer, Encourager, Reader, Reporter, Monitor, etc.?	
Explaining the Task	Write a quick summary and make it as clear as possible.	
Structuring Accountability	How will they (and you) know the task is complete and at what quality level?	
Structuring Group Cooperation	Why should they work together? Is a group format really best for this activity? Are they comfortable with one another?	
Criteria for Success	Exactly what is to be accomplished?	
Specify Desired Behaviors	Tell them how you would like them to interact with one another, not only socially, but academically.	
Monitoring	Plan to move around, listen, and help.	
Providing Assistance	Think of ways you could help groups who get "stuck."	
Closure of Lesson	Link group reports/activities clearly into the lesson and/or lesson summary.	
Assessing Student Learning	What did students gain from the lesson? e.g., " I learned. . ." slips or comments.	
Assessing Group Functioning	Have students share how well their groups worked and what they are learning about working together.	

General Guidelines for Beginning Teachers

Some general rules for starting the year off right:	Things to do before the first day of school:	That first morning:	During the first few weeks:
Be firm but fair from the start. Know your students. Plan your work carefully. Observe other teachers. Start slowly. Establish routines. Set standards. Be patient. Be calm. Do not do paperwork in class. Keep a sense of humor. Accept and try suggestions. Keep up professionally.	Check your administration manual. Know your building. Get to know your supervisors. Make your room attractive. Get materials ready for the first day. Make a temporary room arrangement. Make a program for the first week, knowing you will probably alter it later.	Arrive early. Think over the three tasks you need to accomplish in the first few days: establish room control, set up good work habits, teach group cooperation. Greet students with a smile. Have your name on the chalkboard. Get students right into an activity. Make opening exercises brief. Check attendance. Develop room standards. Follow plans so students will feel they accomplished something the first day.	Maintain management. Study students' cumulative folders. Take advantage of every opportunity to meet parents. Begin a worthwhile class project. Record plenty of observations and grades. Spend sufficient time in lesson preparation: this will seem unusually long at first, but will grow shorter. Take advantage of available help (principal, specialists in the building, media center personnel, district personnel, etc.). Take advantage of professional meetings.

In addition: Think about transitions from one activity/lesson to another, the "short time periods at the beginning and end of the day, before and after recesses, and between lessons" during which "80 percent of classroom management problems occur" (Templeton, 1991, pp. 90–1).

How are lunch money, teacher notes, homework, book orders, etc., to be handled? Can some of the burden be transferred FROM the teacher? Can students begin the day by reading silently or writing in dialogue/buddy journals while the teacher does required business? Are there routines for work collection and materials distribution? What about students who complete assignments? How will you close the day?

Sources:
From INSTRUCTOR magazine. Copyright (©) 1978 by Scholastic Inc. Reprinted by permission of Scholastic Inc.
Templeton, Shane, *Teaching the Integrated Language Arts.* Copyright (©) 1991 by Houghton Mifflin Company. Reprinted with permission.

BRIDGES

Chapter 11
Classroom Order and Discipline

Chapter 11	A. *Personal, Dialogue, or Buddy Journals*	B. *Self-Directed Study Activities*	C. *Cooperative & Collaborative Ideas*	D. *Whole Class*
Introducing the Content	1. **WRITE** about some memories of punishment and/or reward in class and their effects. 2. What motivates you academically? Has that changed over the years?	1. What does the term "negative reinforcement" mean to you? **SKIM** the chapter to see how your definition **COMPARES** with that of the text. 2. **READ** or **SKIM** *Discipline with Dignity* or another management text. What do you think of the major points in the text? 3. **WRITE** an imaginary letter to your students' parents explaining your discipline plan (if you didn't do this for Chapter 10). If you are teaching now (i.e., student teaching,	1. **BRAINSTORM** classroom rules, interventions, and/or situations you recall as particularly effective or ineffective. **CONSIDER** why you think these occurred. 2. **CREATE A SONG** to **SUMMARIZE** either your "rules" or the woes of classroom discipline and management. You may want to try Polette's idea (p. 67) or *Animal Piggyback Songs*.[1]	1. **BRAINSTORM** meanings for the term "negative reinforcement." **EXAMINE** how this differentiation applies in teaching. 2. Introduce this chapter by sharing the poem "Rules" by Karla Kuskin. **BRAINSTORM** with the class several generic rules and consequences. **CONSIDER** natural versus contrived consequences.

Chapter 11 continued	A. *Personal, Dialogue, or Buddy Journals*	B. *Self-Directed Study Activities*	C. *Cooperative & Collaborative Ideas*	D. *Whole Class*
Assimilating/ Reviewing the Content	3. Did you ever break a rule and experience natural consequences as opposed to imposed consequences? How do these differ? Is one experience more effective? For what?	observing, etc.) address it to your assigned grade level. 4. **ADD** management considerations to a previous lesson plan you have written or seen. **SHARE** your changes with your instructor or a small group. 5. **CONSIDER** the three management views discussed in Chapter 11. Have you experienced any or all of them? What implications might your experiences have for your future teaching decisions? 6. Think of a possible classroom rule. Frame it as a fun song or poem that could be used in class to remind students of the idea in a fun way. (See **RULE SONG,** p. 92, for an example.)	3. **BRAINSTORM** cultural experiences relating to management. 4. **ROLE PLAY** for the class an intervention from the 3 perspectives: behavior modification, humanist, classroom management. **DISCUSS** how these differed and what was most effective. 5. **BRAINSTORM** some management "blame" messages. Work in groups to **CORRECT** these messages to "sane" ones. **SHARE.**	3. Obtain 2 copies of the book *Discipline with Dignity* (or another favorite management book) and complete the **READ-A-BOOK-IN-AN-HOUR** activity (p. 92).

Chapter 11: Checking Your Understanding

Match the following terms with your own definitions or summary statements taken from the text:

surface behaviors   intermittent reinforcement   name dropping   conditioning   low-profile classroom control
deflection techniques   internal reinforcement   external reinforcement natural reinforcer   negative reinforcement
anticipation   positive reinforcement

True or False:

1. _____ Students can, in almost all cases, control their behavior if expected and allowed to do so.

2. _____ It is generally best for the teacher to choose the punishment for a misbehaving student since a disruptive student has yielded his or her right to agency and privilege.

3. _____ It takes time to establish a successful classroom routine, so new teachers shouldn't be overly concerned about management issues until after the first month of school.

4. _____ If you are teaching students a classroom rule at the beginning of the year, you should keep teaching it until it is learned.

Multiple Choice:

5. _____ Humanist approaches to classroom management emphasize:
   a. Shared thoughts and feelings of the group
   b. Development of communication skills to influence learners' self esteem and behavior
   c. Immediate behavior changes and compliance
   d. Recognition that group power is more important than individual will

6. _____ Behavior modification approaches to classroom management emphasize:
   a. The idea that behavior can be altered through punishment, reward, and reinforcement
   b. The importance of negative reinforcement to curb avoidance behaviors
   c. The belief that what preceded a behavior is of utmost importance, regardless of what follows it
   d. The need for open communication and "telling"

7. _____ An effective classroom management plan should
   a. Respect cultural differences
   b. Stop persistent misbehavior with strategies simple enough to be used consistently
   c. Create attention seeking and work avoidance behaviors
   d. Quickly and unobtrusively redirect misbehavior once it occurs

1. T   2. F   3. F   4. T   5. b   6. a   7. a, b, and d

Chapter 11: Performance Assessment Ideas		
Individual	*Small Group*	*Whole Class*
1. What are your greatest management concerns? How do you plan to ADDRESS them? LIST 3–5 concerns and 2–3 sources (for each concern) to which you might go to address these challenges if you need more help.	1. Work together in small groups to **CREATE** a poem, lyrics to a song, etc. to **SUMMARIZE** key concepts in the chapter. (See example in **ACTIVE LEARNING** section, p. 92).	1. **BRAINSTORM** potential management problems for a particular grade and setting. **CHART** ways in which each management problem might be handled, **LISTING** the strengths and weaknesses of each choice.

CHILDREN'S LITERATURE CONNECTION

Baumgart, K. (1992). *Anna and the little green dragon.* New York: Hyperion.
  Anna's misbehavior results from a surprise visitor—even though her mother doubts the verity of her claim. This fun version of "The devil made me do it" can spark discussion about responsibility for behavior.
Brown, M. (1986). *Arthur's teacher trouble.* New York: Scholastic.
  Arthur gets the hardest teacher in third grade. What gives "hard" teachers their reputation? Is it all bad?
Carlson, N. (1991). *Take time to relax!* New York: Puffin Books.
  Forced to slow down due to a huge snowstorm, a busy family reconnects and learns to have fun again. Good introduction to the idea of balance in classrooms between work and fun.
Meddaugh, S. (1992). *Martha speaks.* Boston: Houghton Mifflin.
  Martha the dog learns to speak—then learns that with the ability to communicate comes the responsibility for one's words and their effect on others. Students learn this at various ages, and with varying degrees of sensitivity.
Thaler, M. (1993). *The principal from the Black Lagoon.* New York: Scholastic.
  A student fears the visit to the principal, based solely on the principal's reputation (and perhaps the child's active imagination).

SUGGESTED READINGS

Antón-Oldenburg, M. (2000, September). Celebrate diversity! *Scholastic Instructor,* 46–8.
  Antón-Oldenburg shows that what teachers need to know in order to teach successfully in multicultural classrooms has more to do with knowing the values, socialization practices, interests, and concerns of their learners than with knowing about presumed learning style preferences and cognitive styles.
Canter, L., & Canter, M. (1992). *Assertive discipline: Secondary workbook: Grades 9–12.* Santa Monica, CA: Lee Canter & Associates.
  This book, geared primarily for the secondary classroom, presents classroom management from the applied behavior analysis tradition.

Canter, L., & Canter, M. (1997). *Assertive discipline: Positive management for today's classroom.* Santa Monica, CA: Lee Canter & Associates.
   This book focuses on positive classroom management strategies that can anticipate and avoid discipline problems.

Curwin, R. L., & Mendler, A. N. (1997). *As tough as necessary: Countering violence, aggression, and hostility in our schools.* Alexandria, VA: Association for Supervision and Curriculum Development.
   These authors discuss the "school-within-a-school" concept, where some educators are experimenting with subdividing larger groups into smaller subgroups based upon grade levels, special needs, or interests to recognize and resolve conflict in positive ways.

Fisher, B. (1994, August/September). Getting democracy into first grade—or any grade. *Teaching K–8,* 87–9.
   Well-known teacher describes her use of various student committees to manage her classroom.

Glasser, W. (1998). *Quality school: Managing students without coercion.* New York: HarperPerennial.
   Glasser points out that effective classroom managers create a learning environment where students want to be, develop mutually agreed standards of behavior that students must follow to remain in the environment—and shows how to reach these goals.

Harcones, J. (1992). Natural reinforcement: A way to improve education. *Journal of Applied Behavior Analysis, 25*(1), 71–6.
   This article sets out the procedures for transferring the motivation for learning from external reinforcers to internal—or natural—reinforcers.

Jones, F. H. (1987). *Positive classroom discipline.* New York: McGraw-Hill.
   A presentation of many useful techniques for managing your classroom during the first year of teaching.

Levin, J., & Nolan, J. (1991). *Principles of classroom management: A hierarchical approach.* Upper Saddle River, NJ: Prentice Hall.
   A classroom management book that covers the topics of low-profile classroom control and how to deal with "surface behaviors."

Mercure, C. M. (1994, December). Elementary schools' answers to corporal punishment. *Education Digest,* 25–8.
   Shares management strategies from all over America.

Miller, H. M. (2000). Teaching and learning about cultural diversity: All of us together have a story to tell. *The Reading Teacher, 53*(6), 666–7.
   Miller suggests a number of ways teachers can develop "intercultural competence"—or the ability to interact smoothly and effectively with members of various cultures. Among these they include reaching out to others from cultures different than their own to ask for input and insight.

Rich, D. (1987). *Teachers and parents: An adult-to-adult approach.* Washington, DC: National Education Association.
   A resource on the changing role of the family and the responsibility of teachers in creating ties between home and school.

Rinne, C. (1997). *Excellent classroom management.* Belmont, CA: Wadsworth.
   Rinne uses the expression "low-profile classroom control" to refer to strategies used by effective teaches to stop misbehavior without disrupting the flow of a lesson—indispensable skill for any teacher.

Rotter, J., Robinson, E., & Fey, M. (1987). *Parent-teacher conferencing.* Washington, DC: National Educational Association.
   An extensive guide to planning and conducting parent-teacher conferences.

Sparzo, F. J., & Poteet, J. A. (1989). *Classroom behavior: Detecting and correcting special problems.* Boston: Allyn & Bacon.
   An excellent reference for the hard-to-manage classroom and the unengaged learner.

Templeton, S. (1991). *Teaching the integrated language arts.* Boston: Houghton Mifflin, 101.
   Includes some ideas for daily schedule for a self-contained elementary classroom. Ideas can be adapted for other elementary settings and may provide a frame from which to plan your own schedule.

[1]Warren, J. (compiler). (1990). *Animal piggyback songs.* Everett, WA: Warren Publishing.
   Includes a number of lyrics about animals written to be sung to familiar tunes such as "Row, Row, Row Your Boat," etc. A mailing address for this company is P.O. Box 2250, Everett, WA 98203.

ACTIVE LEARNING

RULE SONG
The following rule about not chewing gum in class could be sung to the tune of "Row, Row, Row Your Boat":

> Stow, stow, stow your gum,
> When you come to school.
> Chew it anywhere but here,
> That's a cardinal rule.

READ-A-BOOK-IN-AN-HOUR
Tear out the chapters of a paperback book and distribute them to individuals, pairs, or groups of students. Students read their sections silently or orally together. Students summarize their section orally together and rehearse what they will tell the group (whole class) about their section. (Allow 15–20 minutes for reading and 3–5 minutes for students to summarize the section.) Students may make notes for final presentation. Allow students to present their sections numerically or obliterate section/chapter numbers and have students attempt to place their section/chapter in relation to other sections/chapters presented. If students "guess" where their section falls, have them 1) speculate about content covered in the previous chapter, and 2) predict content in the next chapter when they meet in their groups. Begin the whole class sharing by asking, "Who thinks they have the first section/chapter? Why?" and continue on until the sections/chapters are in order and the book is summarized.

Source: From Bromley *Language Arts Exploring Connections,* 2/e. Published by Allyn and Bacon, Boston, MA. Copyright (©) 1992 by Pearson Education. Adapted by permission of the publisher.

ASSESSMENT ACTIVITY
For example, the following lyrics could be sung to the tune, "Jingle Bells" and summarize some of the chapter concepts:

First Verse:

Dashing through the halls,
Late for class again,
Drawing on the walls with a red felt pen.
Passing notes in class,
Sleeping in their chairs,
Failing to complete their work,
I'm tearing out my hairs!

Chorus:

My students have the best of me—
What am I to do?
I make the rules, they laugh at me;
I feel an utter fool!
Where's the magic remedy for my classroom woes?
It's anticipatory management,
And staying on my toes!

Second Verse:

Group dynamics, growth and change,
This I need to know;
And I need to realize how groups can work
   and grow.
Reinforcement and reward,
Carefully dispensed,
And whenever possible, natural consequence!

Repeat Chorus.

BRIDGES

KNOWLEDGE

**Chapter 12
Assessing Learners:
Objective and Essay Tests**

ACTIVITY

Chapter 12	A. *Personal, Dialogue, or Buddy Journals*	B. *Self-Directed Study Activities*	C. *Cooperative & Collaborative Ideas*	D. *Whole Class*
Introducing the Content	1. **REFLECT** on memories of objective and standardized tests. Were you ever denied something or did you ever receive a grade that was not reflective of your ability/ knowledge? 2. What does it mean to be test-wise? Can that be taught? Should it be taught? 3. **COMPLETE** the **TRADITIONAL PRACTICE QUESTIONS** as an **ANTICIPATION GUIDE** (p. 7) for this chapter.	1. **LIST** your test strategies for the following types of question: T/F Multiple Choice Fill in Short answer/essay 2. Do you see any value in pre- and post-testing? What pros and cons do you see?	1. With a partner, **BRAINSTORM** 3–5 poorly written test questions. **TRADE** your questions with those of another pair. **IMPROVE** the other group's questions. Do a **THINK, PAIR, SHARE** (p. 7) to review the questions and changes. **CHOOSE** one or two good questions and **WRITE** the first and second versions on clear acetate to **SHARE** with the whole class. 2. **BRAINSTORM** with the group the meaning of "mastery." How do you know when some-one has "mastered" something?	1. **DISPLAY** an overhead transparency of a camera. **ASK** students to imagine you sneaking into their apartments at an odd hour of the day or night and snapping a photo of them while they slept. **IMAGINE** blowing it up to poster size and using it to introduce them to someone new, to determine a job application, etc. **ASK** what kind of information this photo would include? What is accurate? Inaccurate? How would they alter the situation to give a more "complete

Chapter 12 continued	A. Personal, Dialogue, or Buddy Journals	B. Self-Directed Study Activities	C. Cooperative & Collaborative Ideas	D. Whole Class
Assimilating/ Reviewing the Content	4. How do you study for a test? What information do you tend to retain after the test is over? 5. What is the relationship between assessment and self-esteem? Should it be this way? How would you alter it?	3. **DESIGN** a test for something in class or something you are/or will be teaching. **REFLECT** on your design and make changes after reading this chapter.	3. **DEVISE** a way (in small groups) you'd like your instructor to "test" you on this chapter. **PRESENT** your idea to the class, along with a rationale supporting it and a method for including it in your course assessment. **CARRY IT OUT** if the class votes to use your idea and **DEBRIEF** on its strengths and weaknesses.	picture" of themselves? **LINK** to the idea of assessment and "one-time" snapshots of a child's performance on a certain task in a certain setting at a certain point. 2. **ANNOUNCE** a pop-quiz. **GAUGE** students' response. **DISCUSS** pros and cons of testing in this manner as well as in other ways. 3. **GIVE** students a test (like **"HOW IT WORKS"** on p. 57). **DISCUSS** the strengths and weaknesses therein.

Chapter 12: Checking Your Understanding

Match the following terms with your own definitions or summary statements taken from the text:

reliability   criterion-referenced test   content validity   validity
accuracy   concurrent validity   norm-referenced test   standardized tests

True or False:

1. _____ Generally, the more items included in a test, the higher the test's reliability.
2. _____ An advantage to "grading on the curve" is that it simplifies marking decisions.
3. _____ The purpose of a test blueprint is to create a format for grading future tests—saving a teacher time and effort in writing tests.
4. _____ Equal differences between percentile ranks indicate equal differences in achievement.
5. _____ One way to reduce the effects of guessing on True/False tests is to require students to correct false items to make them true.
6. _____ When standardized tests originated, it was widely believed that learning ability was inherited, fixed, and largely unchangeable.
7. _____ A good practice for giving essay tests is to write many essay questions and allow students to choose the one they want to answer—enhancing a sense of choice and self-expression.
8. _____ Teachers should avoid using controversial items on essay tests because there is no single right answer.

1. T   2. T   3. F   4. F   5. T   6. T   7. F   8. F

Chapter 12: Performance Assessment Ideas

Individual	*Small Group*	*Whole Class*
1. **INTERVIEW** an instructor about the kinds of tests s/he uses and why. **ASK** for pointers helpful to a beginning teacher. **SUMMARIZE** the results of your interview and **LINK** them to the material discussed for this chapter and/or in your course text.	1. **FIND** an old objective test from this course or another—or **OBTAIN** a test used in grade level/subject you'd like to teach. **EVALUATE** the questions for variety and effectiveness. What do you notice?	1. **OBTAIN** a copy of a standardized test (practice form) used in elementary or secondary schools in your area. As a class, **"TAKE"** the test and then **EVALUATE** both the experience and the questions. **CONSIDER** the types of questions and their validity. What **RECOMMENDATIONS** would you make regarding the use of this test and its results?

SUGGESTED READINGS

Borich, G., & Tombari, M. (2003). *Educational assessment in the elementary and middle school classroom.* Upper Saddle River, NJ: Merrill/Prentice Hall.

The authors focus this assessment text exclusively on the elementary and middle school, providing the pros and cons of objective type assessment formats for these grades and highlighting innovative alternative forms of assessment that work with younger learners.

Farr, R. (1992). Putting it all together. Solving the reading assessment puzzle. *The Reading Teacher, 46*(1), 26–37.

Noted assessment authority offers a short history of assessment in the United States and summarizes the numerous considerations involved in assessment, including assessment audience, purposes, etc.

Glazer, S. M. (1993, January). Assessment in the classroom: Where we are, where we're going. *Teaching K–8,* 68–71.

Discusses the debate over assessment and the role of standardized testing in the schools. Advocates creating a balance between various elements involved in assessment.

Glazer, S. M. (1993, February). Authentic assessment. *Teaching K–8,* 99–100.

Offers guidance for teachers who want to enhance their assessment skills for a better match between curriculum and testing.

Gronlund, N., & Linn, R. (1995). *Measurement and assessment in teaching* (7th ed.). Upper Saddle River, NJ: Merrill/Prentice Hall.

A comprehensive guide for constructing classroom tests, including extensive coverage of both multiple-choice and essay items.

Kubiszyn, T., & Borich, G. (2003). *Educational testing and measurement: Classroom application and practice* (7th ed.). New York: Wiley.

The authors provide a comprehensive presentation, examples and applications of the objective, essay, performance, and portfolio assessment formats along with grade-specific examples of how to use them effectively.

Lyman, H. (1991). *Test scores and what they mean.* Upper Saddle River, NJ: Merrill/Prentice Hall.

Emphasizes the practical use and interpretation of test scores from the teacher's perspective.

Stiggins, R. J. (2001). *Student-centered classroom assessment.* Upper Saddle River, NJ: Merrill/Prentice Hall.

Among other assessment topics, the author covers four objective test formats: true-false, matching, multiple-choice, and completion (short answer). Stiggins prefers the term selected response for these "objective" test formats to emphasize that it is the system by which these formats are scored that is objective and not necessarily the test item.

Thorndike, R. M., Cunningham, G. K., Thorndike, R. L., & Hagen, E. P. (1997). *Measurement and evaluation in psychology and education* (5th ed.). Upper Saddle River, NJ: Merrill/Prentice Hall.

This text devotes extensive coverage to planning, classroom tests, and rules for writing a variety of test items. It also has a thorough treatment of standardized tests.

Winograd, P., Paris, S., & Bridge, C. (1991). Improving the assessment of literacy. *The Reading Teacher, 45*(2), 108–16.

Explains many of the disadvantages of traditional assessments and offers several guidelines to improve assessment.

BRIDGES

Chapter 13	A. Personal, Dialogue, or Buddy Journals	B. Self-Directed Study Activities	C. Cooperative & Collaborative Ideas	D. Whole Class
Introducing the Content	1. What comes to mind when you hear the term "performance assessment?" Have you been involved in any performance assessment? What do you see as pros and cons from a learning perspective? From a teaching perspective? 2. How do you feel about grades? Tests? How would/could you alter the system?	1. WRITE a personal philosophy statement as if for a job application on your philosophy of teaching, learning, discipline, and management. CONSIDER especially issues of assessment: How do you plan to ascertain what students know and what they accomplish? 2. ASSESS yourself on one of the assessments in the referenced articles, or on some areas you choose, such as: acquiring information, organizing it, and using it. What	1. When should you assess learning (i.e., before, during, after a lesson, unit, etc.)? Why do you feel this way?	1. INTRODUCE this chapter with the following quotation: *Give me a fish and I eat for a day.* *Teach me to fish and I eat for a lifetime.* —Author Unknown. ASK how a teacher can know a child has learned something. CONTRAST a performance assess-ment with a paper/pencil test. MAKE THE CASE that testing "how to fish" would be best carried out at a stream with a rod, rather than in a classroom with a paper/pencil test.

Chapter 13 continued	A. *Personal, Dialogue, or Buddy Journals*	B. *Self-Directed Study Activities*	C. *Cooperative & Collaborative Ideas*	D. *Whole Class*
Assimilating/ Reviewing the Content	3. Who should be involved in performance assessment? What do you think should be collected? By whom? Why? When? How often? 4. When should you assess learning (i.e., before, during, after a lesson, unit, etc.)? Why do you feel this way?	implications do these skills have for your teaching career? 3. **CREATE** a self-evaluation rubric related to a particular area of knowledge/ expertise you hope to develop or have developed in this course. **EXPLAIN** why this process is helpful. 4. **COMPLETE** a self-evaluation rubric if you've been keeping a portfolio for this course. Where are your major areas of growth? Where would you like to improve? What kinds of learning experiences appear to be particularly useful to you? Why? What implications does this have for your future teaching decisions?	2. **BRAINSTORM** a rubric for grading the portfolios being used in this class (if that option was chosen). If a rubric already exists, **REVIEW IT** and **SUGGEST** alterations/changes. **NEGOTIATE** these changes with the other groups and the course instructor. 3. **BRAINSTORM** some performance assessments that could be pertinent to this course. What are the strengths and weaknesses of these ideas? If possible, **COMPLETE** some of these ideas.	2. **DISCUSS** primary trait and/or holistic scoring procedures. Work as a group to score some student essays (obtained from a nearby elementary school perhaps). **DEBRIEF** on the experience.

Chapter 13: Checking Your Understanding

Match the following terms with your own definitions or summary statements taken from the text:

rating scales	portfolio assessment	observable performance	rubric
primary trait scoring	objective assessment	holistic scoring	checklists
habits of mind			performance objective

True or False:

1. _____ When creating a scoring system for a performance assessment, the number of points or categories should be limited for ease of use and scoring.

2. _____ It is important to remember that performance assessments are tests and that no learning should occur during the assessment.

3. _____ An area conventional tests have assessed very well over the years is that of student affect and attitude.

4. _____ A well-planned performance assessment presents the learner with an authentic, real-world problem or challenge.

5. _____ Conventional paper-pencil tests are popular because they measure learning directly.

6. _____ One advantage of performance assessment is that it can be used at any point in the instruction process without losing its usefulness.

Multiple Choice:

7. _____ Which of the following is not a common student test constraint to be considered in creating performance assessments?:
   a. time to prepare, revise, finish
   b. equipment such as calculators, computers, etc.
   c. getting help from others
   d. cost of reference materials

1. T   2. F   3. F   4. T   5. F   6. T   7. d

Chapter 13: Performance Assessment Ideas		
Individual	*Small Group*	*Whole Class*
1. **COMPLETE** the final self-evaluation of your portfolio if you have been keeping one during this course. **MEET** with your instructor to evaluate your progress in the course and the value of the portfolio experience.	1. If you have been keeping portfolios, **BRING** them to class and **SHARE** your favorite entries. **DISCUSS** the value of the portfolios as well as suggestions for improvement.	1. **ASK** students to **WRITE** a summary of their teaching philosophy and management plans. **EXPLAIN** to students that this summary is similar to an essay question on many job application forms, making this writing a "real world" experience. **STATE** evaluation criteria clearly before students write—are there concepts or areas they **MUST** address? Is form/mechanics focus a part of the scoring? etc.

CHILDREN'S LITERATURE CONNECTION

Moss, M. (1995). *Amelia's notebook.* Berkeley, CA: Tricycle Press.
   Designed to look like a child's journal, Amelia's notebook lets the reader see the "real" Amelia, typical of portfolio assessment materials.

SUGGESTED READINGS

Anderson, J. B., & Freiberg, H. J. (1995). Using self-assessment as a reflective tool to enhance the student-teaching experience. *Teacher Education Quarterly, 22*(1), 77–91.
   Discusses the value of helping prospective teachers reflect on and evaluate their own performance just as we encourage them to require of their students.
Asturias, H. (1994). Using students' portfolios to assess mathematical understanding. *The Mathematics Teacher, 87*(9), 698–701.
   Discusses why and how to use portfolios in mathematics assessments.
Berenson, S. B., & Carter, G. S. (1995). Changing assessment practices in science and mathematics. *School Science and Mathematics, 95*(4), 182–6.
   Describes use of journals, portfolios, and performance assessment activities.

Costa, A., & Kallick, B. (Eds.) (2000a). *Assessing and reporting on habits of mind.* Alexandria, VA: Association for Supervision and Curriculum Development.

Costa, A., & Kallick, B. (Eds.). (2000b). *Activating and engaging habits of mind.* Alexandria, VA: Association for Supervision and Curriculum Development.

These related books tell you how you can teach and activate thinking processes, attitudes, and social skills in your learners that can prepare them for the adult world.

Courtney, A. M., & Abodeeb, T. L. (1999). Diagnostic-reflective portfolios. *The Reading Teacher, 52*(7), 708–14.

These authors discuss how student input and reflection on how portfolio selections meet (or do not meet) established criteria can be an important part of a successful portfolio or performance assessment project, even for very young learners.

DeFina, A. (1999). *Portfolio assessment (Grades K–8).* New York: Scholastic Trade.

The author shows how the portfolio can be a measure of deep understanding and how it can record growth in competence and understanding across the term or school year.

Farr, R., & Green, B. (1993). Improving reading assessments: Understanding the social and political agenda for testing. *Educational Horizons, 72*(1), 20–7.

Provides a brief history of the evolution of testing to help readers understand current criticism of some of these techniques. Includes a brief recommendation section.

Galley, S. M. (2000). Portfolio as mirror: Student and teacher learning reflected through the standards. *Language Arts 78*(2), 121–7.

These authors show how to link performance assessment with local, state, and national curriculum standards, thereby increasing the relevance of the performance activity for attaining curriculum standards.

Henk, W. A., & Melnick, S. A. (1995). The Reader Self-Perception Scale (RSPS): A new tool for measuring how children feel about themselves as readers. *The Reading Teacher, 48*(6), 470–82.

Introduces an instrument for assessing readers' self-perceptions and sense of self-efficacy, targeted particularly for primary and intermediate level students.

Johnston, P. H. (Ed). (1992). Snow White and the seven warnings: Threats to authentic evaluation. *The Reading Teacher, 46*(3), 250–2.

Suggests seven areas where assessment can be misleading or confusing.

Katz, L. G., & Chard, S. C. (1998). Issues in selecting topics for projects. *ERIC Digest.* Washington, DC: Office of Educational Research and Improvement & U.S. Department of Education. (ERIC Document Reproduction Service No. ED 424 031)

These authors suggest ways in which the teacher can help students select projects and portfolio topics that are worth their time, are intellectually rigorous, and have the potential to extend student interests beyond current study.

Klenowski, V. (2002). *Portfolio use and assessment.* New York: Taylor & Francis.

The author presents an up-to-date text covering many types of portfolios and how you can asses their effectiveness in teaching higher order thinking processes and skills.

Kuhs, T. M. (1994). Portfolio assessment: Making it work for the first time. *The Mathematics Teacher, 87*(5), 332–5.

Offers step-by-step considerations for undertaking portfolio assessment.

Linn, R. L., Baker, F. L., and Dunbar, S. B. (1991). Complex performance based assessment: Expectations and validative criteria. *Educational Researcher, 20*(8), 15–21.
  A clear, concise review of the strengths and limitations of performance tests. Also discusses research that needs to be done to improve their validity and reliability.

Loucks-Horsley, S., Kapiton, R., Carlson, M. D., Kuerbis, P. J., Clark, P. C., Melle, G. M., Sachse, T. P., & Wolten, E. (1990). *Elementary school science for the 90s.* Alexandria, VA: Association for Supervision and Curriculum Development.
  This book illustrates the importance of measuring attitudes or habits of mind in performance assessment as well as understanding and application.

Marzano, R. J., Pickering, D., & McTighe, J. (1993). *Assessing Student Outcomes.* Alexandria, VA: Association for Supervision and Curriculum Development.
  Gives an exceptionally thorough treatment of the dimensions of learning that portfolios can assess and presents numerous examples of scoring rubrics.

Quellmalz, E., Schank, P., Hinojosa, T., & Padilla, C. (1999). Performance assessment links in science (PALS). (ERIC Document Reproduction Service No. ED 435 708)
  These authors show how performance assessments can be applied to the science curriculum, not only to learn science but to think beyond the confines of the traditional curriculum to motivate and aspire confidence in science.

Rhodes, L. K., & Nathenson-Mejia, S. (1992). Anecdotal records: A powerful tool for ongoing literacy assessment. *The Reading Teacher, 45*(7), 502–9.
  Describes the usefulness of anecdotal records and offers suggestions for using them successfully in assessment.

Sgroi, L. A., Gropper, N., Kilker, M. F., Rambusch, N. M., & Semonite, B. (1995). Assessing young children's mathematical understandings. *Teaching Children Mathematics, 1*(5), 275–7.
  Describes how teachers devised assessment activities to coincide with the teaching activities they were using.

Stahle, D. L., & Mitchell, J. P. (1993). Portfolio assessment in college methods courses: Practicing what we preach. *Journal of Reading, 36*(7), 538–42.
  Offers suggestions for using portfolios in college methods classes so future teachers can experience this alternative assessment practice from the "inside."

Tierney, R., Carter, M., & Desai, L. (1991). *Portfolio assessment in the reading-writing classroom.* Norwood, MA: Christopher Gordon.
  A complete book on portfolio assessment which examines pros and cons of the approach and offers concrete suggestions for making portfolio assessment useful and effective.

Tombari, M., & Borich, G. (1999). *Authentic assessment in the classroom: Applications and practice.* Upper Saddle River, NJ: Merrill/Prentice Hall.
  This text is exclusively devoted to projects, problem and project based learning, performance assessment and portfolios that can measure learner knowledge, skill and understanding in life-like learning environments within your classroom.

Wiggins, G. (1992). Creating tests worth taking. *Educational Leadership, 49*(8), 26–34.
  This article provides excellent examples of teacher-made performance tests in a number of different areas.

Wilson, L. (1994). What gets graded is what gets valued. *The Mathematics Teacher, 87*(6), 412–4.
  Suggests that students tend to avoid class activities that don't "count" toward their grades.